Schools of Th

Lessons to learn from schools doing things differently

David James and Jane Lunnon

BLOOMSBURY EDUCATION

LONDON   OXFORD   NEW YORK   NEW DELHI   SYDNEY

BLOOMSBURY EDUCATION
Bloomsbury Publishing Plc
50 Bedford Square, London, WC1B 3DP, UK
29 Earlsfort Terrace, Dublin 2, Ireland

BLOOMSBURY, BLOOMSBURY EDUCATION and the Diana logo are trademarks of
Bloomsbury Publishing Plc

First published in Great Britain, 2024 by Bloomsbury Publishing Plc

This edition published in Great Britain, 2024 by Bloomsbury Publishing Plc

Text copyright © David James and Jane Lunnon, 2024

David James and Jane Lunnon have asserted their right under the Copyright, Designs and
Patents Act, 1988, to be identified as Authors of this work

A catalogue record for this book is available from the British Library

ISBN: PB: 978-1-4729-8846-1; ePDF: 978-1-4729-8839-3; ePub: 978-1-4729-8840-9

2 4 6 8 10 9 7 5 3 1 (paperback)

Typeset by Newgen KnowledgeWorks Pvt. Ltd., Chennai, India
Printed and bound in the UK by CPI Group (UK) Ltd., Croydon, CR0 4YY

To find out more about our authors and books visit www.bloomsbury.com
and sign up for our newsletters

Contents

Acknowledgements

David would like to thank his wife, Yvonne, and his children, Chloe, Emily and Ben, for the support they gave during the writing of this book.

Jane would like to thank Neill, Josie and Jamie for inspiring her every day, and all the friends and family who help keep the show on the road!

Both David and Jane would like to thank Joanna Ramsay at Bloomsbury for her patient, supportive and expert editing and guidance throughout the process and all the colleagues and pupils they are both lucky enough to work with and for every day.

Many thanks to all the interviewees for their inspiring leadership and their passion for education of all kinds: Greg Ashman, Dale Bassett, Katharine Birbalsingh, Alan Bird, Peter Broughton, Jenny Brown, Matilda Browne, Andrew Copson, James Dahl, Dr James Davies, Professor Lise Eliot, Vibe Esdahl-Schou, David Gajadharsingh, Dr Matt Gibson, Bradford Gioia, Will Goldsmith, Jane Herron, Tom Hicks, Conrad Hughes, Pierre Laurent, Sir Ian Livingstone, Simon Lockyer, Graham Macaulay with Phillip Hedger, Dr Richard Malpass, Aamena Mayet, Alistair McConville, Laurence McLellan, Leslie Medema, Jon Needham, Neill Oldham, Sarah Raffray, Dominic A. A. Randolph, Dr Millan Sachania, Jaskamal Singh Sidhu, Clare Wagner, Mandy Watts, Ian Warwick and Stuart Worden.

Introduction

How can schools as large, highly structured environments meet the varied and complex needs of the students they teach? Can particular unifying, coherent sets of priorities make it easier for schools to operate effectively, and if so, how? How much can and should schools' values or priorities change over time in keeping with societal norms?

In this book we talk directly to leaders from a wide range of schools to find out how – and why – they focus on what is important to them and why they favour a core idea, or approach, over other competing demands. Both of us have worked in schools for over 20 years and we take it for granted, to some extent, that we know how schools operate. We started to think: How much do we hear, directly, from other schools with very different approaches? We wanted to talk to school leaders working in schools with a clear sense of identity, that meet a deep-seated need from the students and families they serve, and the communities they work in. We wanted to talk to schools in the UK and overseas, state-funded and fee-paying, and give them a platform to talk about how they sustain the visions they have shaped and promote in these demanding, changing times. In each chapter we hear from several schools who are powerful proponents of particular focuses or approaches. In the same chapter we also hear from someone who holds an alternative view and we pose questions throughout to promote discussion and reflection.

We spoke to 30 school leaders across eight countries whose schools are to some extent defined by a unique philosophy or ethos. While the focus of this book is not to analyse the cultural implications that might come about when interviewing teachers from different countries, it is worth considering that there may be cultural or historical factors at play which might have an effect on the responses given. They are schools that have thought deeply about how to not just deal with complex issues, but to thrive as a result of them. Each chapter explores an issue which is not just wide-ranging, but under constant discussion within and outside schools: faith schooling, single-sex schooling, traditional and progressive approaches, creativity, curricula and assessment, use of technology and approaches to wellbeing. Each can be divisive but, approached in the right way, can also be transformative and empowering. We talked directly to a school's headteacher or senior leader, and they provided information for the fact files which give additional context for each discussion. But we also wanted to add a different, and informed, perspective on these contentious issues, so at the end of each chapter we include 'Another View', written by leading figures who are engaged in the debates we have explored with our school leaders. In doing so we hope greater balance is added to complex, and often polarising, issues. In addition, there are 'Reflections' which discuss the interview content and the views proffered to promote debate and reflection.

We realised that although we have a lot of experience as teachers, and although we had strong opinions on each of the issues discussed in this book, our experiences of schools dealing directly with such areas is, inevitably, limited. You may have a strong opinion about faith schools, but how many have you visited? You may passionately believe in the necessity of a traditional education, but what does that mean in practice in the classroom, and how does it prepare young people for the modern world? The more we asked questions the more we realised how limited our experiences are. Teachers know their own schools very well, and they will have a knowledge of other schools they have worked in, have sent their children to or are governors of. But it is rare to find anyone who has visited and talked to leaders in depth in more than a dozen schools in their career. Even for a school inspector, it is stretching credibility to say that they see schools as they truly are when they are inspecting.

Schools are very busy places, and the heads, or deputy heads, we talked to are under huge pressure. Anyone who has worked in schools knows that just dealing with 'stuff', both expected and unexpected, takes up most of the working day, and so designing an agreed strategic development plan that is fully supported and implemented by all takes a huge effort. Having a philosophy, or mission statement, that is meaningful and goes beyond the platitudinous is nothing short of Herculean, and each of the schools we talked to do this. They have distinctive ideas that they believe in, and we wanted their voices to be heard. We realise that visiting schools and talking to headteachers, staff and pupils is an experience that is beyond the scope of most people, including those, like us, who work full-time in schools. We hope that this book is the next best thing: an opportunity to listen to those working on the 'front line' of learning, doing the best they can to give the children they work with the best possible outcomes. There is no doubt that working in schools has become increasingly difficult over the last ten years. Social media, greater political scrutiny and funding crises, not to mention a global pandemic, have imposed exacting demands on everyone involved in primary and secondary education. The leaders of the schools we talked to have not only worked with colleagues to cope with some, or all (and more), of these demands, but have thought through a coherent set of principles that, they feel, strengthen their schools. That they can do so says a great deal about the resilience of the staff in the schools themselves, but also the depth to which these beliefs are held. We hope you enjoy hearing about each of these schools and that it in turn creates and informs thoughtful debate and reflection.

Chapter 1

Faith schools

In England, approximately a third (34%) of all state-funded schools (DfE, 2019a) are faith schools. What can faith schools offer to pupils which other schools cannot? What might the drawbacks be? In this chapter we talk to faith school leaders and gain their insights into the strengths and challenges of a faith-based education, as well as hearing an opposing view.

As we will read about in this chapter, for proponents of faith education, it represents enrichment and spiritual nourishment designed to set children on a clear spiritual and moral path for the rest of their lives. But for others working in secular establishments, there may be questions. Grappling with adolescence may be challenging for many young people so should they also be expected to grapple with questions around faith? Does attending a school that defines itself through its faith add, rather than remove, complexities? Perhaps the intensity of growing up can be made more difficult, as well as more understandable, when seen through the prism of faith.

Faith may not be something consistent, permanent or unquestioned. Faith may often be most challenged by those who possess it most deeply. Sarah Raffray, the former head of St Augustine's Priory, sees her 'faith journey' as 'just that – like lots of people it wanes and becomes more fervent or rich at different times'. Aamena Mayet, the principal of Eden Girls' School, would agree. She talks openly about how some of her students question their faith and explains that it can be part of growing up. For the heads of such schools, these could be seen as brave admissions.

For some, faith schools may seem like closed-off, inward-looking institutions, intent on focusing on their religion to the detriment of a broader understanding of life and society. Faith, for some people, may be seen as the cause of conflict, rather than an answer to strife. With this in mind, what can faith schools offer families living in an increasingly secular society? Should faith override all other considerations? How important might it be to parents to choose a faith school that adheres to their own values or beliefs, particularly against other factors such as academic results and future university and job prospects? Might those who do not support the concept of faith schools create any barriers for those who do attend faith schools, or send their children to them?

The faith schools we talked to represent four of the world's religions: Christianity, Islam, Sikhism and Judaism. Two are fee-paying schools and two are state schools. All are based in the south east of England. We were interested in what approaches they shared, how their differences were made obvious because of their faiths, and what they felt they gained, and lost, by being faith schools.

We asked each of the senior leaders at these faith schools the same set of questions. In doing so, we wanted to see what similarities and differences emerged, and how these were an articulation of the school's faith, as much as they were personal to the school leaders themselves. We wanted to explore what the senior leaders believe to be the importance and strengths of faith schools, what challenges they face, and how important faith is for the parents. If a school has a strong faith identity, to what extent does that force any school leader's own vision into something secondary?

St Augustine's Priory

Fact file

Number of pupils: 475

Age range: 3–18

Co-educational/Single sex: Single sex (girls' school)

Location: UK

State-funded/Independent: Independent

Faith: Catholic

When was it established? Originally a foundation of the Augustinian convent of the Canonesses Regular of the Lateran in Paris in 1634, it moved to London in 1911, and then to its current location in Ealing in 1915. It offers a Catholic education to girls.

Head/Contributor: Head: Christine Macallister; Contributor: Sarah Raffray (headteacher until March 2023)

Our pupils come from: The school's intake is ethnically diverse. 40% of pupils identify themselves as Catholic. The school has children from other faiths, as well as those with no faith.

Our values: Our girls and staff have the courage and appetite to tackle everything that life throws at us. We educate girls in the Catholic tradition and this means that students leave us rooted in values that make them effective in their personal and professional lives.

Our academic vision: We aim to ensure that girls leave St Augustine's equipped with the full range of skills required for lifelong success as women.

Our pastoral vision: We want our girls to change the world because they are ethical leaders sowing joy, truth and courage. Among other qualities, the school cherishes love for our neighbour and welcoming different faiths and cultures. By learning through dialogue, we have hearts open to the whole world.

The importance of faith

Until recently most heads of Catholic schools were from a religious order – nuns or brothers or priests. The first generation of lay heads had that institutional memory to work with; second generation lay heads, like me, have to do a lot of work to find what is called the *charism* [the defining spirituality] of whichever order founded the school.

St Augustine's has only two nuns alive now – they are in care homes and they have withdrawn completely from the school. I find inspiration from the founding stories of the school. I learned this approach from the other Catholic schools I have worked in. Over time as a leader, it has become less about my personal faith and more about the charism or particular influence of the founders. St Augustine's was founded in recusant times – in France in 1634 – so we have an incredible heritage which gives an authentic set of values and resonance for today.

Our identity is about that heritage – in our case, women of courage, for whom religious freedom mattered more than life. These days, the secular agenda attacks us constantly, not least because people think to be secular is neutral while to be Catholic is somehow dodgy. I think this is dangerously flawed. Our school history posits that there is something greater, something transcendent – some purpose we all have. Catholic teaching speaks of 'imago dei' which means 'made in the image of God'. This means that each one of us is unique. One of my mantras is to say to the pupils: Look at your hands – there is only you on this earth with those fingerprints. It is also about courage, about women of faith using their voice for others – one of the first nuns in Ealing was a suffragette who tied herself to railings outside Downing Street. We teach each pupil that she has some unique purpose on the earth. We remain counter-cultural.

Because I wholeheartedly espouse the values of the school's heritage, I can express these values without reservation, and having been at St Augustine's for 10 years I can also see how, even during my tenure as head, we have refined and recast our mission statement to reflect newer times while staying authentic to who we are. But we have to stay within canon law and we are inspected against an Ofsted framework for this. This is exacting educationally and in terms of ethos – it challenges us profoundly and is why, while my faith matters, what is more important is to be a head who understands how to speak to these matters in a way which is compelling and which balances some of the real challenges which Catholic doctrine poses to a 21st century way of life and school. That is why constant formation for me is vital – so I have the knowledge, language and conviction to explore some of those real tensions, whilst making sure I don't ever break canon law. Since the pandemic, a new inspection framework for Catholic schools has been launched. This has felt like poor timing at best. As fewer families attend mass, more is being asked of Catholic schools and it can feel, more than ever, that we are rowing against the times. People don't want to be hectored. They want compassion, especially when it comes to matters of sexuality. I know many headteachers who are struggling with what feels like a pharisaical [a strict observance of religious conduct] approach. The law of the Church seems to matter more than love, which is what has always drawn me. As Catholic leaders, we are encouraged to follow the example of Christ. He turned over the tables in the temple in righteous anger. Headteachers of Catholic schools are drawn to matters of social justice and we can't help roaring at ideology which appears counter to those teachings!

The strengths of a faith school

As a faith leader, I can help students navigate their world – hopefully modelling the way in which the Word of God, at so many levels, is a comfort and inspiration. At its most literal, the Bible as literature is a fantastic text and underpins so much of an understanding of Western civilisation, including the arts and philosophy. It is arguably important that our students recognise the intertextuality of its references.

We don't force anything but we offer stillness – an ability to be in total silence, often with others – in a way that is at ease with peace. Fundamentally, we believe in a God of love. At a time when so many people are seeking care, gentleness and kindness after the trauma of the pandemic, we are not afraid to say to pupils that we love them. This is quite radical, but it has a profound impact on them.

We are founder members of the London-based Faith and Belief Forum – founded with a Jewish school and a Muslim school. In the early days a toolkit – RADIO – was created to enable proper learning, especially when exploring highly emotive topics like abortion.

RADIO stands for:

R – Respect

A – Active listening

D – Dialogue not debate

I – Where am **I** in this? (I do not speak for all white Catholic women, for example.)

O – **O**ops (apologise) and **O**uch (I am offended/upset by that)

This toolkit has come into its own when we have worked with our whole community to discuss moments when issues of race and religion have been especially prominent and some have felt that their foundational beliefs or identity have come under attack.

We have now adopted the toolkit across the school from Early Years to parent meetings – it helps young children call out microaggressions in the moment and it helps grown-ups to apologise. Oddly, the childlike language gives people permission to do this more directly.

This toolkit drives our Inclusion Committee. We balance different beliefs and feelings – the unequivocal stance of Catholic teaching on LGBTQ+, for example, and the strength of feeling some Muslim students can have against the passion of those students for whom the LGBTQ+ agenda is vital (quite literally in some cases) to staying alive. We have arrived at an extraordinary place, where we have deeply sophisticated conversations and where the pupil voice is the thing I am most proud of. I think this works in our context because all students' knowledge about religion is properly informed and not superficial. GCSE RE is compulsory, and importantly, students are not allowed to give one view in the specification – they have to show both sides of the argument. I fear that those who don't have this knowledge or academic discipline miss out on great depth.

We are 40% Catholic and most other families join us because their faith tradition matters hugely to them. For us, a trite treatment of Islam is not good enough, just as writing off all Catholics as being allowed to do what they fancy because they go to confession trivialises something which is taken very seriously. And is, in fact, a profound misunderstanding of it.

The challenges of a faith school

A huge challenge is being held to account by two inspectorates – especially when the Catholic inspectorate seems to be increasingly granular in telling schools what they can and can't do. For example, we are not allowed to wear rainbow badges. The tensions in the Church are palpable and extremely painful – and serious. I have felt muzzled – if I am not allowed to wear a rainbow badge because it signals allyship, then how do I assert to my pupils that whatever their sexuality, they are welcome in this place, and more than that – that they are loved? A group of headteachers was recently told that this teaching was Truth. I struggle with this and I know many others do too.

The importance of faith to parents

As religious education is core to who we are, and we ask everyone to participate in our faith life, parents are supportive. Some struggle. For some, we are not Catholic enough, for others we are too Catholic. Some Muslim parents want the all-girls, single-sex element of our education and they support our avowed espousal of our faith, but they worry that their daughters learn too much of the Catholic faith. But we welcome all traditions and our Muslim parents are fantastic at sharing the importance of their faith with us.

Catholic parents no longer feel they must educate their children in a Catholic school, and so while it is helpful, it is just part of what they are looking for. That is a shift even in the last 15 years or so. The people we do attract are those who work for very values-based companies, companies which are ethically driven or just very culture driven. They recognise that our culture is extremely strong and they find that attractive, even if they are not particularly religious. Where it becomes a tension, is that we set those values at a very high bar and so if we fail in some respect, we can smash to earth very painfully – perhaps more so than if they had never expected us to be quite so bold about what we were claiming we could do. Because we proclaim that we love their children, that we will tackle injustice, if we then fail to manage a situation where there has been some bullying, for example, parents are even angrier than they might have been. Bullying is rare, but we are not forgiven for it when it happens.

The universal bit of being catholic, with a small c, is that when families arrive from India, for example, who were often educated by nuns (even if not Catholic), they walk down a corridor and feel at home. They see statues, the Chapel, polished corridors, and they feel safe. (As long as they had a good experience. The disaster of clerical abuse means the reverse is also true – however, those with terrible experiences rarely come near us.)

Immanuel College

Fact file

Number of pupils: 690

Age range: 4–18

Co-educational/Single sex: Co-educational

Location: UK

State-funded/Independent: Independent

Faith: Jewish

When was it established? 1990

Head/Contributor: Dr Millan Sachania

Our pupils come from: North-west London

Our values: 'Torah im Derech Eretz' (Torah in the Way of the World).

> **Our academic vision:** To stretch every pupil to achieve beyond their expectation.
>
> **Our pastoral vision:** To instil in every pupil a sense of self-esteem and the confidence to project their authenticity.

The importance of faith

Faith is the bedrock of Immanuel College's values and is both critical and central to its identity. It is manifested through representation at senior leadership and middle management levels: we have a deputy headmaster in charge of ethos. The school was founded by the Chief Rabbi in 1990, so its very identity and existence are predicated on the orthodox Jewish faith. That said, Immanuel College today can be characterised as a secular school with a very strong faith focus. The spirit of Judaic experience and religion flows through the school daily. Faith identity is also manifested through the timetable and calendar, i.e. the school is closed for religious holidays and there are school expectations with regard to prayer, food and dress code.

The strengths of a faith school

The benefits are arguably game-changing. All our staff aspire to enable their charges to discover who they are as human beings. To do that, pupils have to understand where they come from. And the school's faith identity means that at Immanuel there are numerous opportunities to explore collective and personal heritage. These opportunities include inspection of the traditions and beliefs that have engendered their families' thinking and experience. All this directly – perhaps beautifully – affects the way individuals connect with themselves, promoting a degree of spiritual understanding which non-faith schools, arguably, cannot provide to an equal extent.

Faith, in the broadest sense, can be hugely beneficial. On a general level, faith identity in school can provide alternatives and challenges to social trends and norms. It allows pupils to look at themselves differently. On a specific level, faith teaching and learning cover a variety of methods and pedagogies. For example, Jewish learning is predicated on paired work with students covering a central text, but encouraging and eliciting their own interpretations.

In fact, it could be argued that the faith dimension of Immanuel College encourages and enables more discussion and dialogue amongst our pupils compared with more secular environments, promoting a culture where pupils constantly challenge and interrogate. Immanuel's students encounter myriad interpretations of rabbinic guidance and learning, and they are not shy of exposing any argument to its moral, intellectual and practical weaknesses, nor of ensuring that the precepts of good Judaic life are extended to peoples beyond the Jewish faith. Such activity exemplifies the role of faith as a vehicle for reflection, debate, examination and the development of individual thought and interpretation as a result of high-level thinking.

The challenges of a faith school

It is essential to find opportunities for pupils to encounter other world views and faiths, and constantly to create opportunities for a dialogue with difference. Equally essential is the promotion of divergence and diversity. The ethos of a faith school must encompass a range of observance and traditions, and ensuring that the enterprise of the school celebrates and embraces this difference, in turn extracting creativity, energy and innovation from such diversity, is a challenging, but worthwhile and fascinating, exercise.

The importance of faith to parents

All parents who send their children to the school will have, on some level, an appreciation of faith-based education. They are broadly supportive and often very actively engaged with their child's faith-based learning. The College is clear with parents both before and during their child's time in the school about what the school's standards and expectations are with regard to its modern orthodox ethos: that is the identity of the school and the leadership enforces it. Boys at school wear a kippah (cloth cap) during the day, for example. If parents are not happy with this prescription, they should not be sending their child to the school. But we ensure that our red lines are reasonably few. And we entirely accept that outside school, pupils and families may well not be conforming to some aspects of the faith lifestyle that we honour in school. That is fine. We do not ask for that. But we do ask that all attending the school, and all parents sending their children to the school, respect Judaism. There is always a spectrum in terms of parental faith – and we do our best to assert the few, non-negotiable red lines and then, beyond that, to respect the preferences of all.

Parents certainly care about examination grades, but an increasing number are prepared to overlook a graded course at (I)GCSE in favour of a more intensive skill-based course in Jewish Studies. In general, the more religious a family outside of school, the more they are prepared to follow this approach. Any tension between the two will largely be in the form of internal debate within the school as to the best approach.

Guru Nanak Sikh Academy

Fact file

Number of pupils: 1,602

Age range: 11–18

Co-educational/Single sex: Co-educational

Location: UK

State-funded/Independent: State-funded

Faith: Sikh

When was it established? The first iteration of Guru Nanak Sikh College was founded by Sant Baba Amar Singh Ji and officially opened in January 1993.

Head/Contributor: Jaskamal Singh Sidhu (Executive Principal)

Our pupils come from: We serve our local community in Hayes, Middlesex. The vast majority of pupils are of Indian heritage, almost all speaking Panjabi at home.

Our academic vision: To provide a quality education that is broad, balanced and relevant to the needs of pupils within a modern society. To enable all pupils to achieve their potential through the highest standards of teaching and learning. To encourage every member of our community to invest in lifelong learning and personal development.

Our pastoral vision: To build a strong community based on the Sikh religion. To develop each pupil's self-esteem, confidence and independence, with consideration for others and the concept of Sewa (selfless service). To strengthen bonds between home, community and school, providing a preparation for each pupil's entry into the wider community.

The importance of faith

As you may know, the word Sikh translates to 'a learner'. Sikhs worship the word of the Guru, knowledge, which they believe is scribed in the holy scripture, Guru Granth Sahib. Sikhs believe that to be a good learner, one must have a healthy soul, healthy body and healthy mind. Guru Nanak, the first Guru, established the foundation of Sikhism with three principles: Naam Japna (meditate in the name of the divine), Vand Chhakna (share with others) and Kirt Karna (work hard and honestly). So, the Sikh philosophy encapsulates spirituality and divinity within the message of the Guru and discipline in form of the code of conduct. The third aspect of the life of a learner is service to others, known as Sewa. The combination of these elements helps Sikhs to make good choices, leading them to live a complete life.

At Guru Nanak Sikh Academy, we believe that these principles, when put into practice, help us to create strong learners who are ready to contribute positively and earnestly to the wider community. We believe that education is a tool that can help us to eradicate poverty. Poverty is not always in monetary terms: it could be a lack of knowledge leading to ignorance of some serious issues that humanity is facing today, such as discrimination, inequality, conflict and hatred, among others.

Our values stem from Sikh philosophy and help us to focus on the key purpose of education: creating a better world.

We are a dynamic learning community, always adapting and seeking new ways to enable our students to tackle the challenges of an ever-changing world. We take pride in the inclusive nature of our curriculum. The student voice plays a significant role in the key decisions. Based on student voice, the academy has implemented gender-neutral uniforms and unisex toilets.

The strengths of a faith school

Pupils have a strong sense of community and service which they derive from our values and principles. Our pastoral team holds one assembly with each year group every week, which is focused on celebrating successes and promoting our values. Students also have one religious assembly each week, which is led and organised by a team of student volunteers. Students appreciate the fact that education and attaining knowledge are not the goal but are instead the tools to achieve the ultimate objective of creating a better world.

The Sikh faith is the foundation of the identity of our school. The name, values and practices stem from Sikh beliefs. We believe the Sikh way of life is a great way to become a good learner. Our SHARE values are the driving force for our community, which also reflects the concept of 'a good learner'. SHARE is an acronym that stands for Sewa (selfless service to others), Humility, Achievement, Respect and Equality. Our values are reflected in everything that we do. They are embedded in our strategic development plan and symbolise the significance of the character of our school. We have a Gurdwara (a place where Sikhs come together for congregational worship) on-site where students assemble in the mornings to perform prayers and start their day with a message from the Guru. This has been a practice since the beginning of the school in 1993. A positive start to the day with mindfulness and meditation is excellent for our students.

One of the strengths of our approach is that it helps our students to become well-rounded human beings who are prepared to contribute to their society in every way. They develop academically, socially, morally, emotionally and spiritually throughout their journey, which makes them stronger from within and more capable of facing the uncertainties of life.

Guru Granth Sahib is seen as a secular scripture meant to be a spiritual guide for the whole of humanity, and this is reflected in our school's values. The Sikh holy scripture has the writings of different faiths and denominations within its compilation. Being a Sikh faith school does not restrict us in any way but helps us to embed a secular perspective in our practices.

The challenges of a faith school

[Please note that the content here focuses on how the school addresses challenges rather than the challenges themselves.] I see challenges which, if not tackled by the faith school leadership wisely and thoughtfully, will potentially become drawbacks for them. Like every establishment, faith schools have their challenges, which can most certainly be beaten.

As a faith school, we have clearly established our purpose and vision, which guides our community in all aspects [of school life]. The school vision has to be aligned with the purpose of education and the legislation. Religion strengthens and shapes our emotional and spiritual state. Education develops well-rounded, happy and skilled citizens ready to contribute to and support the society where they can collectively prosper. Understanding the purpose and the balance of the two aspects are necessary to fulfil their objectives.

Our school leaders are well-equipped to prevent any misuse of religious sentiments from promoting anti-social or harmful feelings in youngsters. They are aware of how these feelings can reach students from social media and other channels, and work in parallel and consistently to make them aware and educate them against them. Our curriculum is designed to instil compassion, kindness and responsibility in our students, contributing to their personal and social wellbeing.

As an outward-looking school, we are always seeking to provide opportunities for our students to grow a better understanding and knowledge of the world. We have ensured that our curriculum offers our students enough opportunities to have diverse experiences inside and outside the classroom. Local and international trips play a significant role in achieving this objective. As with any other school, we want our students to develop an inclusive, respectful and supportive approach to life. So, it becomes vital to provide the opportunities for them to interact with diverse cultures, beliefs and practices so they can learn how to respect the diversity in our society.

Our vision, values and ethos help us to hold strong in the direction in which we want our students to lead and become role models for all of us. As I said, the challenges are easily defeatable and easier to handle when the vision is well-aligned between all stakeholders.

The importance of faith to parents

Most of our students come from Sikh families. We have students from other faiths and some non-faith families, and in my experience of 17 years in this school, I have only seen parents supportive of the values and ethos of the school. Parents encourage the school management and the board of directors to do well in promoting the Sikh faith and values, and they contribute actively to celebrating Sikh festivals so the children can understand the significance of Sikh history and feel proud of their roots. Parents have very high academic aspirations for their children and they are always involved in their child's school life. The relationship works well because there is a good understanding that the child's spiritual and emotional health has a direct impact on their education and academic achievements.

The world is more divided than ever between the 'isms and 'ists. However, religion plays a significant and positive role in establishing a much-needed culture in a secular society. Religion has been, and will always be, a moral compass for the majority of people in our society, and faith-based schools can help young children to develop positive and respectful attitudes, and foster a culture of mutual understanding and tolerance. Respect for all and promoting equality has always been the mission of every religion. Faith-based schools are the flag bearers for a diverse and fair education system where parents have the right to choose a school that aligns with their religious beliefs.

Eden Girls' School, Waltham Forest

Fact file

Number of pupils: 612

Age range: 11–18

Co-educational/Single sex: Single sex (girls' school)

Location: UK

State-funded/Independent: State-funded

Faith: Islamic

When was it established? Our school was founded in 2014 and is part of the Star Education Trust.

Head/Contributor: Aamena Mayet (Executive Principal)

Our pupils come from: Eden Girls' School is a non-selective girls' state school located in east London. The vast majority of pupils are of

Asian heritage and almost all are speakers of English as an additional language.

Our values: Service – being a responsible citizen in our community; teamwork – working together for excellence; ambition – aspiring to be our best; respect – treating others as we wish to be treated.

Our academic and pastoral vision: The school aims to 'promote a culture of educational excellence, from within a caring and secure Islamic environment enriched with the values of discipline, mutual care and respect, which extends beyond the school into the wider community'. The vision contains three key elements: educational excellence, character development and service to communities. The school's vision is to nurture 'today's young people and inspire tomorrow's leaders'.

The importance of faith

Faith underpins every aspect of our school. It is explicit from the moment you walk in. In fact, it is there before you walk in: it is reflected in our logo, the octagonal star. It is expressed through subtle influences throughout the day. Each lesson begins and ends with a prayer, for example.

For us, the most important thing is that our pupils foster a confident identity as British, Muslim Londoners. That's what our school seeks to achieve.

The strengths of a faith school

Our faith gives us a clear set of values and a belief system on which the entire school is predicated. And we are fortunate that the Islamic tenets intertwine so closely with universal values of humanity.

For example, a key pillar of Islam is to give back: to focus on charitable work. We believe that our faith acts as a force for good in the local community and in the wider world. Nobody questions that in our school. And we are very big on this kind of work. (For example, we have a large number of cake sales; a lot of cake is eaten in these buildings!) Indeed, our pastoral calendar is focused around charitable events. And in 2021/22, we raised £28,000 for charity – that was despite COVID-19 and the fact that 38% of our pupils are on pupil premium funding. That's amazing.

It's also very useful to be able to refer back to our faith when there are behaviour concerns. It gives us a common language. For example, if there are girls who are not working hard enough, or with enough focus, we can use the well-known Islamic prophet's saying: 'Tie your camel'. This refers to a teaching of the Prophet Muhammad (peace be upon him) of the man who said 'I leave my camel in God's hands.' The Prophet replied, 'Tie your camel first, and then leave it in God's hands!' The point is that we all have our own responsibilities which we should acknowledge and accept willingly, and we should not leave too much to our god. Being able to use the phrase 'Tie your camel', with everyone understanding what that means, is one of the great benefits of a shared faith. Staff equally need to 'Tie their camel', and it's incredibly useful to have those universally understood values and a shared frame of reference.

We also take our pupils on faith trails. [Faith trails are walking tours that take you to different places of worship in a town or city.] We talk a lot about the commonality of belief. We were one of the schools, working with British Futures [a UK-based charity whose aim is to educate people in equality and diversity], selected to host Holocaust memorial services last year, for example.

The challenges of a faith school

Of course, there are times when teenagers can have a crisis of faith. We recognise that they are on a journey and there are no hard-and-fast rules about when people will feel what. When that happens, we are not insistent. We will, instead, be gentle; suggest books or passages that they might find helpful to read.

There is always the possibility for tension between faith and educational outcomes. But we have worked hard to try to anticipate and resolve those. For example, we have timed our school day to facilitate the faith needs of many of our families. Our day begins at 8.00, not 8.15, for example. This means that our girls are not travelling when lots of other kids are travelling to schools close to us in the area. This is useful, because kids can misbehave. It also means that for those pupils whose parents want them to be schooled more specifically and in more detail in the Muslim faith after school, this can easily be achieved. These are practical solutions that are rooted in our faith. Similarly, we dismiss our girls and staff earlier on Fridays – we finish at 12.10 and have a two and a half day weekend so that the girls and staff can attend Friday prayers. Again, this is a practical – and welcome – initiative which supports our families and staff.

People have preconceived ideas about Muslim schools, and that can be hard. But we have rigour and place academic matters at the heart of what we do. We are not unquestioningly deferential: things have to work for us.

The importance of faith to parents

There is always the challenge of meeting the demands of parents: for some, we are not conservative enough. Equally, we have parents who say [they are not as] focused on the praying aspect [and are] interested in [us] providing the best education, which of course we do.

Some parents can get over-focused on the wrong things in our view: too much conversation about the colour of the hijab or a concern that we are over-egging British values in our teaching. But we come back to what we are about: this is a school aiming to empower and educate girls and young women, growing up as Muslims, in east London. We are a school with attitude and parents get used to that. We are very open about that. We tell them that we are nurturing tomorrow's leaders and providing them with business opportunities: debates, partnerships work, drives on STEM (science, technology, engineering and mathematics), working with GCHQ (Government Communications Headquarters), focusing on cybersecurity and a whole host of other things.

For us, [faith] can underpin our conversations with parents too. For example, if a child is disrespectful or rude to or about a parent, in their company, we are absolutely part of the reinforcement, as our faith teaches us that: 'Heaven lies underneath the faith of your mother.' We have found ourselves in a position where we get to remind the pupils of that and their parents very much appreciate it!

Another view

In this section, Andrew Copson strongly presents various perspectives that counterbalance those of the contributors above. He discusses not only the right of parents to choose how their children are educated but also the rights of children themselves to have as balanced an education as possible, whether that is within a faith school or not.

Andrew Copson, Chief Executive of Humanists UK

Under the European Convention on Human Rights, parents have an explicit right to bring up their children in the religion or belief of their choice without illegitimate interference from the state. However, that does not extend to a right to demand state funding for confessional religious teaching or for religious schools that are in line with those beliefs. We live in an increasingly diverse society where, consistently, over 50% of the population has no religion (Clery et al, 2016). It is unfair for the state to engineer the school system to fund or promote one religious belief over another, or to exclude children from their local school due to the religion (or lack of religion) of their parents. What's more, parents' rights must always be balanced with the needs and interests of children who have their own right to freedom of religion or belief, independent of their parents. If a child is sent to a school that endorses and reinforces only the same ideas as the parents at home, the child is deprived of genuine education, which includes being exposed to ideas and beliefs and values of different kinds.

Many private and illegal [unregistered] faith schools provide inadequate education (Humanists UK, 2020a) – and there's a strong moral case to oppose that. However, many faith schools perform well in assessments and school league tables (The School Run, 2023).

The problem is that all the evidence shows this 'high performance' is largely down to religious selection – which also acts as a proxy for selection by factors such as parental wealth and ethnicity – rather than anything special about a religious ethos (Leckie and Goldstein, 2019). Religious schools assist in segregating our society; they work against equality of opportunity and, by teaching about religion from one perspective, violate freedom of religion or belief.

Diversity of thought within schools is surely what is to be applauded and encouraged. This is because education in all schools should be critical and objective, and I think it is inappropriate for any school to promote a particular world view or treat one such perspective as true when issues are not settled but a matter of opinion. So, I would not support the idea of a school providing humanist instruction.

There is little evidence that parents gravitate towards faith schools simply because they're faith schools: parents want the best for their children and therefore they like good schools. This is natural. In many areas, good schools appear to also be faith schools – not least because their discriminatory admissions privileges have been shown to perpetuate economic and social divides.

In 2021, an Ofsted survey found that 94% of parents of school-aged children did not consider the faith-based affiliation of a school to be one of their top three factors in choosing a school. (Ofsted, 2021a). In 2022, the Office of the Schools Adjudicator (OSA) argued that faith schools disadvantage vulnerable children (OSA, 2022), and in 2021 Humanists UK concluded that faith schools routinely deprioritise children who are, or were, in care in their admissions policies (Humanists UK, 2021a). In 2020, Humanists UK gave evidence to Liverpool City Council showing that faith schools' admissions policies disadvantaged the non-religious, ethnic and religious minorities, and the poor (Humanists UK, 2020b).

Increasingly, parents are being allocated faith schools against their wishes (Humanists UK, 2021b) and this problem looks likely to grow as the proportion of people identifying as non-religious increases. Recent figures from the Church of England show that there are now more places in Church schools than in the Church's entire 'worshipping community' (those who attend regular religious services) (Humanists UK, 2020c). On this basis, it is the continued support for faith schools that is untenable.

Furthermore, [applying to] religious schools can lead to parents exaggerating the extent of their religious observance in order to secure a place in a specific local school, which devalues religion itself.

Suffolk Council recently voted to end religious discrimination for admissions to 35 Church of England schools, and this new policy is likely to be popular with parents – Suffolk's own polling found that 68% of respondents, mostly parents, agreed with the change (National Secular Society, 2022). This is broadly in line with attitudes across the UK: three quarters of parents disagree with religious selection in state-funded schools (Accord, 2012).

I should add that phrases like 'teaching of religious faith' often need further clarification. There is a vast difference between proselytising or religious instruction on the one hand, and, on the other hand, teaching children about the history and present state of different religions and world views in a critical and objective manner. I believe the former is wholly inappropriate in state-funded schools and should take place voluntarily and outside of school hours; the latter is essential.

My ideal secondary school would be open to all children irrespective of their religion or belief, with an objective, critical and pluralistic curriculum that includes teaching about religions and non-religious world views such as humanism. School assemblies would be an opportunity to bring the school community together and would be educational, enjoyable and appropriate for young people from all backgrounds. Education would focus not just on inducting children into all the diversity of our human heritage but on developing them as critical thinkers, engaged citizens and fulfilled individuals.

I would say to parents: choose whatever you think is best for your child. Parents have to balance a range of factors when selecting a school so, as long as they consider the rights and interests of their child, it would be unfair to ask for any more. The fault lies not with parents but with the system.

Reflections

Is faith, as a connection to tradition and heritage, accessible in the same way in secular environments?

All of our contributors commented on this point with passion. It can be argued that the different faiths connect us to humanity's roots and our contributors spoke repeatedly of the 'wider family' and 'chain of tradition' to which they belonged. Faith may provide perspective and context and the contributors reflected with an openness and insight on the reassuring connection that a faith ideology can provide.

In our interactions with the leaders of faith schools interviewed, their belief in the logic and anchoring power of a faith-based philosophy came across very strongly. It was clear in all these schools that they felt that their assertion of belief, of values, of a moral code, provided a clarity around what really matters to them. And with this came a restfulness and assurance which underpinned our conversations (with students and staff alike). Certainty, constancy and connection are powerful themes and could be viewed as rare currency. One can see why this part of a school's identity may attract parents who might be seeking safe environments in which their children can thrive.

But it is also possible to see why others might think that, in Andrew Copson's words, faith schools 'assist in segregating our society'. Copson argues that 'they work against equality of opportunity and, by teaching about religion from one perspective, violate freedom of religion or belief'. Some of our school leaders acknowledged that they have to ensure that their pupils remain broad-minded and critical of intolerant views. As our contributor Jaskamal Singh Sidhu states: schools should 'develop positive and respectful attitudes, and foster a culture of mutual understanding and tolerance'.

Is faith a vehicle for high-order thinking, debate and interrogation?

Another point which recurred in our discussions and school visits was the sense that providing a tight, even sometimes rigid, belief system, within which the identity and operation of the school sits is, paradoxically, and perhaps ironically, a great way of generating high-order analysis, questioning and debate. Pupils, we were told, almost invariably engage critically, at some point, with the tenets presented by their school. As Dr Millan Sachania put it, 'Ironically, [attending a faith school] leads to a greater capacity for questioning dialogue amongst pupils because questions arise… they simply didn't arise in the same way in the secular schools I've worked in…'. Contributors held that the process of reflecting on and wrestling with ancient theological traditions or tenets, and relating them to the experience of being an adolescent in the 21st-century western world, creates pupils who are very used to thinking critically and independently. They felt that pupils may be more confident in articulating their views and participating in questioning dialogue with their peers and with staff because they are at a faith school. Interviewees suggested that the very fact that questions arise so frequently in faith environments means that the children benefit from the process of grappling with them and finding answers together. For the school leaders we spoke to, faith can be seen as a common ground – a shared language and set of experiences that can be discussed, debated and accepted, and which goes to the core of collective and individual identity.

This is perhaps a surprising position to hear from staff representing faith schools, but it is an intriguing one. Embedded in this assertion is a suggestion that many of the practices and approaches in a faith environment may feel counterintuitive to young people. Contributors suggested that there is a tension between the proclaimed identity of the school and the prevailing social context of many of the pupils, no matter what their background. The pupils we met were almost universally fluent, impassioned, articulate and persuasive on the subject of their beliefs, regardless of their age or background. As the pupils at Eden Girls' School pointed out, 'Our school faith is not restricting. We are always connected and we know what we're doing and why we're doing it. So we get to find ourselves and explore our religion, not in a mosque, but in the everyday.' They were also open about those who did not connect so strongly with the faith: 'I know someone who saw how we prayed at this school, she's at this school and she's now an atheist. The school has encouraged her to think for herself. She was a Muslim because her parents were, but this school helps you think about why you follow a religion and for what purpose.' Perhaps such independence of thought and action is the untold story of faith schools.

Does faith provide a 'safe space' for pupils to explore identity and tough social questions?

Our interviewees felt that a faith school can provide a clear identity to students regardless of their personal or familial faith identity outside of school. They also felt that the faith school context may provide a safe forum for students to explore a faith identity within the school that can stay with them long after their school days are over. The powerful and moving account from a former student of Guru Nanak Sikh Academy, Dr Randeep, testified to this. The values that are at the heart of Sikhism and which were embedded into his consciousness through the daily practice at school of singing 'Deh Shiva', directly influenced his response to COVID-19 and helped him make sense of a period of great challenge and his own identity during that time, in an immediate and explicit way: 'I've been training for this moment… it's my duty to provide care, to provide assistance, even in the face of risk, and in fact especially in the face of risk.' This could be seen as a positive example of the long-lasting impact of the rituals, rhythms and beliefs that underpin many faith schools. One might ask how school leaders can ensure that assemblies that are 'educational, enjoyable and appropriate for young people from all backgrounds', such as Andrew Copson invokes, have the same lifelong resonance.

The school leaders we spoke to argue that faith provides a safe, emotionally powerful roof, under which young people can test out who they are and find their truest, most secure self. Jaskamal Singh Sidhu spoke strongly about that, referencing the power of the student voice in implementing gender-neutral uniforms and unisex toilets. In his school, he felt faith has not been a straitjacket but a liberator – a place of greater safety where identity can be perhaps more fully and openly explored.

The discussion around the 'Tie your camel' proverb with staff at Eden Girls' School provided an appealing insight into the shorthand which a strongly held, universal faith can provide when managing attitude and performance – with staff as well as with pupils. It could be argued that there is something direct and compelling about these shared narratives and assumptions, which perhaps also allows for more time to be spent reflecting on the more existential or difficult philosophical and ideological issues.

Above all, it felt clear from conversations that attendance at a faith school, and daily engagement with the practices that make up the school's routine, is an emotional choice as well as an intellectual one. The pull of a faith education system is strong for our interviewees and runs very deep, perhaps because they see it as based on mutual belief and trust between and across a community.

Pupils cannot know how they will feel later in life, nor what they will then believe. But we had the sense from the contributors that, at its best, the experience of education in a faith-led environment can almost transcend that. A number of the contributors suggested that the important point was to provide children with the emotional confidence and ability to reflect upon and question both oneself and the world to make their own considered decisions into adulthood.

Childhood and adolescence are periods of physical and emotional growth and change during which young people might explore, push against or embrace a myriad of evolving thoughts and beliefs. While schools aim to provide a safe and nurturing environment in which children can explore the most profound questions we face as human beings, our contributors would assert that faith schools provide an additional facet of spiritual engagement upon which to hang these questions. Whether this gives children additional security and structure, or whether it creates additional questions, is at the heart of this debate.

Chapter 2

Single-sex schooling

Most schools in the world are co-educational, and there are many who refer to the old adage that because life is 'co-ed', so must schools be. But what about single-sex schools? What might they offer and is there anything that any school, single-sex or co-educational, can learn from them? Loren Bridge, who served as the Executive Officer of the Alliance of Girls' Schools Australasia before it merged with the International Coalition of Girls' Schools (ICGS), argues that 'life might be co-ed but it is not co-equal' and a number of interviewees highlight the opportunities that single-sex schooling can bring. Many may also feel that single-sex schools can allow space to focus on oneself and on one's learning, rather than on appearance or image – another point argued by Bridge. This chapter will explore what single-sex schools in today's world can offer and the lessons we can learn from them.

Into this mix comes the complex and sensitive discussion around gender identity. Clearly, for all schools, single-sex or co-educational, the whole question of how gender is defined is important to consider. It is a debate that will continue into the future, and it is one that is so complex that it is beyond the scope of this chapter, and indeed this book. Although these questions need to be acknowledged and addressed in schools with staff, students and parents alike, this chapter will not be able to do justice to these important topics, but instead focusses on the insights gathered from a range of interviews.

Historically, the education of girls and boys in single-sex contexts is an ancient and familiar area of controversy. Experts and non-experts alike have long argued over whether there are innate differences between the sexes which require different approaches to teaching them, as well as different areas of interest to engage them. Whilst biology is often presented as the primary explanation for differing characteristics between the sexes, in fact, we ascribe (or project) different characteristics to each sex, and we do so for a number of reasons: personal, political, religious, historic and social. What is true? As far back as 1810, the philosopher Sydney Smith, writing his *Advice to young ladies on the improvement of the mind* (p. 54), stated:

'A great deal has been said of the original difference of capacity between men and women; as if women were more quick, and men more judicious – as if women were more remarkable for delicacy of association, and men for stronger powers of attention. All this, we confess, appears to us very fanciful... As long as boys and girls run about in the dirt, and trundle hoops together, they are both precisely alike. If you catch up one half of these creatures, and train them to a particular set of actions and opinions, and the other half to a perfectly opposite set, of course their understandings will differ, as one or the other sort of occupations has called this or that talent into action. There is surely no occasion to go into any deeper or more abstruse reasoning, in order to explain so very simple a phenomenon.'

Smith may have regarded this as a simple phenomenon, but even in modern times, the argument that when it comes to gender, nurture dominates (and explains) nature, continues to be debated everywhere, from social media, to daytime television studios, in schools and in universities. Indeed, it has become, in recent years, a particularly hot and contentious topic in education and beyond it. Simon Baron-Cohen, Professor of Developmental Psychopathology at Cambridge University, has recently written that 'the female brain is predominantly hard-wired for empathy, and... the male brain is predominantly hard-wired for understanding and building systems' (cited in Fine, 2010, p. xix). Such views might be supported by many of the readers who turned Jordan Peterson's *12 Rules for Life* (2018) into an international bestseller, or who bought John Gray's *Men Are From Mars, Women Are From Venus* (1992) in their millions. Others would challenge such assumptions. Professor Lise Eliot (2019), who contributes to this chapter, has written about the 'gendered brain' and that any hard evidence to support the idea that men and women are fundamentally different *because* of neurology has 'failed to materialize'.

Gender stereotypes seem to stubbornly persist in even the most liberal and progressive societies, arguably with damaging consequences. In her book *Delusions of Gender* (2010), Cordelia Fine observes that the categories of 'male' and 'female' do not seem to be limited to genitalia. For Fine, there are implicit societal associations that link men with careers in science, mathematics, and high authority; whereas women, in contrast, are more closely associated with the liberal arts, family, domesticity and low authority.

Much of the above could make a powerful case for co-educational schooling. The argument might go as follows: give a girl the same opportunities as a boy in a non-selective school, teach them the same subjects in the same way, and there is, presumably, a better chance of establishing a truly meritocratic society.

Maria Gray and Emily Shirreff, founders of the Girls' Day School Trust (gdst.net) in 1872 argued that it was essential for girls to widen the scope of their interests, in order to begin to not only meet their own ambitions, but also to fully understand those around them:

'When [women] learn to extend their sympathies beyond the drawing-room or the nursery, to all that affects the well-being of their fellow-creatures, – when the treasures of knowledge are opened to them with all the wonders of the past and the hopes of the future, and they are able to take an interest in all that is worthy to excite the interest of rational beings, – when they study and appreciate their own position as affecting, and affected by, wide social relations, and perceive the magnitude and importance of the duties it imposes, they will feel that the trammels which seem hopelessly to fetter them are in great measure removed, and that the narrowness of the outer existence cannot, in active minds, confine the free life of thought and feeling.' (1850, p. 16)

The Girls' Day School Trust and other early pioneering girls' schools, such as The Mary Erskine School, James Allen's Girls' School, Cheltenham Ladies' College, North London Collegiate School, Roedean School and Woldingham School were established to allow just this to happen. The aim was to provide a full education, with a broad, challenging, roughly equal curriculum to boys, as part of the political and social fight for female equality. For this reason, these schools were partly defined by what they weren't (namely, a boys' school) and, as discussed in the interviews below, to some extent that perception persists, and can still be a source of strength for girls' schools today. It is hard to imagine in the classrooms of the United Kingdom today the fight for equality that has preceded this style of learning, or that in many countries this fight continues.

The 1880 Education Act making education compulsory for all children aged between five and ten years old, the granting of female suffrage in the United Kingdom in 1918, the gradual opening of all universities to women from the 1860s to the University of Cambridge's eventual late capitulation in 1948 and the passing of the Sex Discrimination Act in 1972 were all significant events in changing girls' and women's rights in the United Kingdom. What then is the ongoing need for girls'-only schools in these contexts? If they arose out of a struggle for girls to be educated on an equal footing to boys, then why do they persist?

What about the argument for boys'-only education? The oldest boys' schools, such as Beverley Grammar School, The Pilgrims' School Winchester, Warwick School, Abingdon School and St Paul's School, were founded in a world which only educated boys, because only boys needed to be prepared for the jobs that only men were able, at that time, to do. If that was their raison d'être, how have they continued to exist for so long in an increasingly diverse, 'co-educational' society?

The question is an important one. Education (from the Latin 'educare' – to draw out) should surely enable us to burst free from the fetters in which we have been born, whatever they are. Why do some see single-sex education as beneficial and a key tenet within which other educational decisions will be made? Single-sex schools may have met an historical need, but how prepared are they now for the societies in which they currently exist? What educational battles are still being fought in single-sex education?

Most of our interviewees for this chapter are supporters of single-sex schools who have opted specifically to work in this sector. (While some of the discussion touches also on the pros and cons of co-educational schools, it should be noted that all interviewees teach in single-sex schools so the perspective is arguably positively biased towards single-sex schooling and focuses on exploring what this can offer.) We asked them a range of questions including what they felt was important about single-sex education in general, what made the single-sex school ethos of their particular school distinctive from their perception of the co-educational school ethos, and what they considered to be the future of single-sex education generally.

Westminster City School

Fact file

Number of pupils: 800

Age range: 11–18

Co-educational/Single sex: Single sex (boys' school) except sixth form which is co-educational

Location: UK

State-funded/Independent: State-funded

When was it established? 1877

Head/Contributor: Mr Peter Broughton

Our pupils come from: All areas of London but predominantly south-east London (40%+)

Our values: Wisdom, integrity, compassion and excellence

Our academic vision: At Westminster City School, we are committed to providing a curriculum that enriches and empowers. We provide an abundance of knowledge and opportunities, meaning our students are able to confidently participate in the great conversations of society.

Our pastoral vision: Westminster City School is committed to teaching all young people how to become exceptional and engaged citizens. We have clear and high expectations of all of those in our community and our collective approach is rooted in four core values – wisdom, integrity, compassion and excellence. At Westminster City School we work hard, we care for each other, we support everyone.

In the future: We wish to be the 'go-to' boys' secondary school (with a mixed sixth form) in London.

The importance of single-sex schools

The pupils gain by having teachers and leaders who think carefully about the impact of gender on a range of different pedagogical and pastoral elements and are intentionally trying to ensure opportunities that reach beyond the societal expectations of (in our case) boys. The school gains specialisms in so many areas of school life. I think there is less volume of modern research on this than might have historically been the case. So, the evidence base is thinner than I would like.

Many Christian families (especially from West African heritages/Caribbean heritages) are very welcoming of single-sex schools and I think other ethnic groups also really value this form of education. That said, there are some compromises. The school loses out on the ability to show some aspects of real life as the world beyond secondary education will never be divided legally by gender. And perhaps the pupils also lose out on seeing the impact of their gender in an immediate way.

Fundamentally, I think parental choice is vital. It matters that there are a range of options available for parents. Overall, numbers of single-sex schools are less important than ensuring there are enough of these types of school in every locality. Some areas of the country (not London) really lack this choice, which is not a positive thing. We are one of two boys' schools in Westminster and this choice is appreciated.

How is the school's ethos shaped by being single sex?

Our ethos is rooted in the Christian faith and it is about supporting, transforming and moulding a group of young men who break the norms, challenge stereotypes and are not limited by their surroundings or backgrounds. In a fully co-educational school, there are fewer opportunities to challenge or transform in a way that a single-sex school must (by being less common).

The fact that we are a single-sex boys' school definitely shapes our assessment and feedback within teaching. Encouraging boys to embrace lower-stakes testing; that is really vital. Equally, encouraging the boys to focus less on the outcome and more on the process is a significant challenge, but one which definitely shapes our teaching.

Similarly, in a pastoral context, being single sex is massively significant for us. It gives the opportunity to work hard on breaking the view that 'boys will be boys', challenging the Andrew Tate style of misogynistic, toxic masculinity, encouraging boys to share emotion rather than bottle it up until it explodes. Moving from bravado to brave resilience is a constant focus for the pastoral team and it is the way we 'do' pastoral care.

The future of single-sex schools

There are certainly challenges ahead in this space. The intersectional boundaries of race, gender, sexuality, religion, class and cultural expectation are fraught and fragile at the best of times. Channelled through social media, in an uncertain time, where the social glue is less adhesive than one would wish for, it is a significant challenge which requires brave and sensitive, but not precious, leadership!

City of London School for Girls

Fact file

Number of pupils: 805

Age range: 11–18

Co-educational/Single sex: Single sex (girls' school)

Location: UK

State-funded/Independent: Independent

When was it established? 1894

Head/Contributor: Jenny Brown

Our pupils come from: All around London and the south of England

Our values: Respect, responsibility and resourcefulness

Our academic vision: Our students will be academically curious and resourceful, will take risks, be ambitious and love learning for its own sake. We want our pupils to be inspired to find their space to pioneer by being given the freedom in almost all lessons to explore, discover and create tasks for themselves, while being encouraged to do so by supportive, highly challenging teaching.

Our pastoral vision: Our students will understand themselves, be listened to, take reflective ownership of their lives and be considerate of others.

In the future: We are focusing on being pioneering in the areas of curriculum space, digital spaces and our physical spaces. We want to ensure equality of access in all three of those areas.

The importance of single-sex schools

Single sex, or co-ed? I think I'd always want to talk about the best of both worlds when considering single-sex and co-ed schools.

The business of any great school is to help students discover first what it means to be human; a long way behind that, it is to consider what it means to be a particular gender. Perhaps the single most important thing a school does is to encourage pupils – boys and girls – to look beyond and outside of themselves. It is only by immersing oneself in knowledge and learning about what is bigger, brighter and better than oneself, that one can truly find oneself and work out what you are and what you might become.

At City of London School for Girls, we are fortunate and unusually placed in that whilst we are a girls' school, we are also part of the City of London Corporation family of schools. Our close links with other schools, particularly with our partner school, the City of London School, a ten-minute walk away, ensures that our students regularly look beyond and outside. Pupils from both schools benefit hugely from the resources available from our two iconic sites in the Barbican (CLSG) and Thameside (CLS). So, in responding to this issue, I can talk about the perhaps unique experience of a single-sex education at CLSG combined with all the value of a pioneering and very close partnership with CLS. This, in effect, creates a form of single sex /co-educational hybrid education for our pupils, which I would advocate.

Of course, gender does have some relevance and it does impact. If I were to make some terribly wild and therefore probably indefensible generalisations, that require both caution and caveat, I would say that girls tend to internalise, while boys externalise, their feelings and behaviours. There are often differences in their learning – in what texts or topics they are likely to find conducive – and how they respond to praise and criticism. They can socialise differently – at lunch and beyond – and will view sports – and sports kit – in distinct ways. The development of girls' self-confidence and self-esteem can often require a different kind of nurturing to boys'. As girls and boys develop at different rates, girls are often capable of longer lengths of concentration during adolescence than boys. As an English teacher, for example, I have found nothing beats the excitement and sophistication of teaching A-level English to high-ability girls. Their ownership of text and level of literary analysis is very different to that of boys at that stage and is incredibly inspiring. Girls often need to be encouraged to please less; boys, to please more.

So, what does a single-sex education offer girls? There is evidence that it benefits girls in terms of growing their confidence and their leadership skills and giving them plenty of room and space to find and own their voices. And they can have a wider breadth of provision and opportunity at single-sex schools; all of the opportunities are there for them alone, not shared with boys, whose needs, particularly through adolescence, are, in many ways, quite distinct. Inevitably then, teaching styles reflect the fact that my staff are operating in a single-sex environment. There is less need for teachers to be engaged in behaviour management, more need for them to work on confidence building.

How is the school's ethos shaped by being single sex?

None of the factors I've referenced above primarily determine the ethos of our school, nor the success of our pupils. Other factors – our values, the quality and motivation of our people, our location and resources – are much more important to the ethos of our school. Pupils here enjoy being at CLSG and parents value it, but not principally because of its single-sex status. In this sense, the gender of our pupils is largely incidental to our success.

This is unsurprising. The most important condition for success is that pupils are in a great school and a great school is not great because of its gender make-up; it is great because of its ability to get the best out of its pupils – whatever their gender – and to instil in them a love of learning, a love of ideas and the ability to think critically, and learn productively with others and play happily with those around them.

Pastorally, of course, things are very different from the past, in terms of what a single-sex education involves. There is an important responsibility for single-sex schools to ensure that there is plenty of co-educational opportunity. Most single-sex schools I know (and nearly all young people attending single-sex schools) have continual access to and interaction with peers of the opposite sex, often through productive collaborations with other schools. For example, at CLSG we have all sorts of combined activities with CLS and that really matters in terms of pupil experience. From a co-curricular point of view, for example, multiple plays and concerts take place jointly with the boys' school. From boys v girls netball matches to joint leadership and entrepreneurship programmes with local companies like Schroders or Linklaters, or our weekly combined general studies and enrichment classes every week for sixth form, we are making sure that students learn in co-educational contexts. We run joint community projects, including for example, joint support of IntoUniversity, where pupils from both schools mentor younger pupils from other schools. Fundamentally, we aim to ensure that much of our 'real world applied learning' happens collaboratively, either with CLS or with pupils from the other City of London Corporation family of schools.

And we have built this into our leadership and management of both schools. Our senior management teams now work closely on strategy together and we have regular formal meetings and training together. In fact, all the teaching and support staff, across both schools, meet annually for joint inset. What this means is that the commitment to the value of partnership percolates through both institutions. What we celebrate is that while all our pupils can benefit from both shared (co-educational) space and learning, they also have their own distinct single-sex spaces and provision. That's what is unique about our approach to education and our set up – perhaps it's a 'best of both worlds' approach to the gender question!

And that's useful too in terms of combatting some of the prejudices that come along with a girls-only education, especially in highly academically selective girls' schools, like ours. One is the phrase 'hot house', which is used a fair bit. In my experience, however, this generally just means you have pupils who are bright, keen to learn and do very well, but in an environment that is warm and highly supportive.

There can be a fair amount of generalising around the mental health of girls in a single-sex setting. If girls are more inclined to perfectionism, however, just as boys might be more inclined to misbehave, these issues are not compounded by being in single-sex environments. Far from it. Being in a single-sex environment means problems are more likely to be recognised and mitigated through the kind of tailored, expert pastoral support which can come from staff who have deep experience of educating one specific sex.

The other prejudice that I think needs tackling directly as a matter of priority is that girls somehow need less space or that it is legitimate to resource girls' education differently, whether in single-sex or co-ed schools. This view and practice is still widespread, but it should be as objectionable as paying female and male staff differently. Why on earth would girls need less space, or to have less money invested in them?

The future of single-sex schools

There is much to be said for the benefits of a co-education for primary aged and post-adolescent pupils. Co-education at primary means that pupils learn to cooperate with both sexes from an early age, leading to mutual understanding and respect for each other. In this way any incipient gender stereotypes are broken down.

It is not unreasonable to expect that in 20 years or so there will be very few solely single-sex schools in the UK. That said, I suspect it will take a while before single-sex education disappears completely. And my reflections from the point of view of a parent, as well as a head and a teacher with long experience of both co-education and single-sex education, is that it takes a long time to fully move a school from being a single-sex or even a majority single-sex institution to a properly culturally co-educational one.

The key question for me for any newly co-ed school, is: 'Is it really co-ed?' Are the sexes equal in every way, or is this still culturally a single-sex school which has brought in the other sex? The culture of a boys' school was not designed for girls at the outset, nor will it have been aligned to the needs of girls for most of its history, so a move to co-education means that everything will need to be substantially rethought. The changes need to be properly established and embedded. All of that takes a long time. Plainly then, any set-up which is predicated on, or ends up having, one gender in a minority, runs the risk of those pupils feeling that they only partly belong in that school; and a sense of belonging is critical in school.

To that end, of course, the question of gender identity is also relevant. Despite what some commentators say, I don't think the shifting views on gender have affected single-sex schools very much. Of course, it is important that schools follow all equality and anti-discrimination law and make judgements consistent with their obligations under the Equality Act, based on informed decisions about the fit for each pupil in a school. But fundamentally, every good school – whether single-sex or co-ed – seeks to look after every pupil as an individual, meeting their needs and providing an environment in which those individuals can thrive and learn, whatever their identity or journey towards selfhood involves. To end then where this reflection started: that's absolutely our job – and our privilege in fact!

City of London School

Fact file

Number of pupils: 1,045

Age range: 10–18

Co-educational/Single sex: Single sex (boys' school)

Location: UK

State-funded/Independent: Independent

When was it established? 1837

Head/Contributor: Alan Bird

Our pupils come from: All across London: we are a commuting school, and we have a diverse pupil body from a range of races, ethnicities and religions. Our bursary programme ensures that the school has a broad range of socio-economic backgrounds amongst its pupil body as well.

Our values: Kind, aware and ready

Our academic vision: We aim to always provide an education in the broadest sense, considering academic excellence with exceptional pastoral care, framed by an outward-looking and forward-thinking approach.

Our pastoral vision: We cherish individuality, shun stereotypes and encourage every pupil to be the best version of themselves. Every member of our community is keenly aware of their responsibility to make a difference. We want to develop kind, respectful and inquisitive leadership.

In the future: We aspire to be a school that prepares respectful, optimistic and inquisitive boys for the rapidly changing demands of the 21st century.

The importance of single-sex schools

There are excellent single-sex schools and excellent co-educational schools. A key principle in any good school is that every single pupil should be treated as an individual: hence pastoral care and the approach to teaching and learning should be appropriately individualised and nuanced. Any broad-brush comment about 'teaching boys' is therefore going to be overly generalised and lack nuance. Indeed, some of the generalised comments that I have often seen don't fully chime with my experience in boys' schools. To give but one example, we think in great detail and (I hope) with great sensitivity about how to support young people who are suffering with anxiety and stress, or who need tailored support to build appropriate levels of self-confidence. These are not issues that are unique to girls' schools. Whilst it might be true to say that, for example, tapping into a competitive spirit is more likely to be an appropriate teaching strategy in a boys-only environment, even this cannot be taken for granted: no two class groups are the same, and the job of an excellent teacher is to develop and use strategies that work for the pupils in front of them at a given point in time.

What a pupil gains from any school is driven by a range of factors, and its single-sex/co-educational status is but one of these. Certainly, a single-sex environment removes a potential source of pressure for young people, as they navigate an increasingly complicated world with more sources of pressure, from which it is evermore difficult to disconnect. That can be of real value.

How is the school's ethos shaped by being single sex?

Our school ethos is defined in the strategic vision (the academic vision referenced in the fact file). The principles at the heart of that ethos are not related to our single-sex status: celebrating diversity and individuality; ensuring that individuals are included and respected for who they are; being outward-looking, and understanding our ability to make a positive difference to our community; enjoying the process of learning for its own sake… All of these themes, which feature prominently in our strategic vision, are not a product of being a single-sex school.

We are fortunate, though, in combining our single-sex status with membership of a wonderful family of schools, which ensures that our pupils engage with young people from a broader set of institutions. Within this, we have a particularly close relationship with our partner school, City of London School for Girls, which is ten minutes down the road. Much of our co-curriculum, our supra-curriculum, our universities and careers guidance, our PSHEE (Personal, Social, Health and Economic Education) programme, our leadership and charitable work, alongside a weekly enrichment programme for the sixth form, is organised on a co-educational basis, and ensures that co-educational activity is embedded within our curriculum. This model means that we can seek to exploit the very best of both approaches (e.g. in determining whether a particular part of the PSHEE programme is best delivered in a co-educational or a single-sex setting). And there is an appetite to see this partnership grow.

It is also worth emphasising that this partnership extends beyond the educational experience of our pupils, and sees our teachers and leaders working increasingly closely, to learn from each other and to benefit from broader perspectives.

The future of single-sex schools

Parents should have a choice, and I therefore welcome the existence of both single-sex and co-educational schools. That said, for our parents, our single-sex status is very much just one factor in their choice of CLS for their son, and it is often not the most important factor.

Montgomery Bell Academy

Fact file

Number of pupils: 835

Age range: 12–18

Co-educational/Single sex: Single sex (boys' school)

Location: USA

State-funded/Independent: Independent

When was it established? 1867

Head/Contributor: Bradford Gioia

Our pupils come from: A radius of 50 miles in the Nashville area.

Our values: Gentleman, scholar, athlete. These values are prioritised in this order. We have spent much time on reinventing the concept of the gentleman value in 21st-century terms. Concepts related to kindness and respect and compassion and empathy have been of greatest interest. Essentially, we want to build boys to be better men who understand that strength can mean vulnerability and putting others before oneself.

Our academic vision: Strong preparation through a classical curriculum that is nimble to incorporate new ideas. We preach the values of hard work and discipline. We want our students to be curious and open-minded. We have built in many opportunities for our students to earn grants to travel domestically and internationally. We have ten exchange programmes. We frequently bring in a diverse range of speakers to offer educational perspectives.

Our pastoral vision: To express care and knowing one another. We have a strong advisory programme. Faculty meet with their advisees every day.

In the future: We want to stay adept to change and to teach boys that they can defy the traditional stereotypes of masculinity and become better men and people.

The importance of single-sex schools

Boys tend to be more open to expressing themselves in the classroom and personally. They are on the whole more engaged in realms like art and music, theatre and debate. They show great care and compassion for one another. There is an ethos of working hard and being as excellent as possible; respecting others, regardless of interests. In a boys' school, the pupils are more open and vulnerable and expressive. Single-sex schools must be more intentional about respecting women and not fall prey to a culture of 'boys will be boys'.

Obviously we must work harder to teach boys to collaborate and to work equally and supportively with girls and women. We have a tremendous opportunity to invent a greater sense of masculinity and to inculcate boys with stronger values.

How is the school's ethos shaped by being single sex?

We work with the International Boys' Schools Coalition. Most of our staff have attended and presented at workshops. Boys appreciate authenticity, strong connections and openness in the classroom. We have studied these methods. I am an advocate of single-sex schools, but I believe culture defines a school community more than being single sex or co-educational, or private or public. There are opportunities to convey the strengths of a single-sex school in all schools. And there is a good case to be made for the opportunities of a single-sex school. Our parents see the values we embrace and believe in the opportunity to be in a strong and cohesive community.

Our staff have learned that boys are more active learners. They relish the opportunities to see boys embrace hard work and discipline and openness in their ideas and interests. We have a great culture of caring for boys. When we hire a staff member, we speak directly about the importance of knowing and caring for the boys. I often say you might be a talented physics teacher or soccer coach, but most of all, I care about your interest in the boys.

The future of single-sex schools

Single-sex schools have been under attack since the 1970s. Inclusivity can mean for some people that single-sex schools are counterintuitive to the right culture and kind of society. We must continue to make the argument that we offer a great opportunity for boys and that our values can be shared with co-ed schools.

Identity politics and the culture wars include issues that challenge us. We must display our respect for these issues and be open to criticism, but we should also be forthright that this option for education is important and transformative.

Henrietta Barnett School

> **Fact file**
>
> **Number of pupils:** 800
>
> **Age range:** 11–18
>
> **Co-educational/Single sex:** Single sex (girls' school)
>
> **Location:** UK
>
> **State-funded/Independent:** State-funded

When was it established? 1911

Head/Contributor: Contributor: Clare Wagner: Headmistress 2021 – 2023 (NB. current Acting Head is Mandy Watts).

Our pupils come from: A wide range of backgrounds. A strong proportion of children are from ethnic minority families, particularly from Indian/Sri-Lankan backgrounds. About 50 languages are spoken at home. Our pupils come from all over London, we have a broad catchment and a number of our children travel a long way. About a quarter of our children live within a three-mile radius and we do favour close locality as part of our selection process.

Our values: We champion girls' education and we are a highly selective grammar school, with a traditional curriculum, educating women for the 21st century.

Our academic vision: We are unashamedly academic and scholarly.

Our pastoral vision: We are a very kind, warm and friendly community. Behaviour is excellent. We promote kindness and mutual respect. We are all supportive of each other, partly because of our small site at the top of the hill. Everyone here is 'held' – there is mutual friendship and support and respect.

In the future: We are really proud that we produce so many girls who pursue STEM subjects, but we also want to ensure the humanities and arts flourish in our school. We are educating women for the 21st century, but within that, we are seeking to encourage the arts and STEM as a genuine grammar school. And we have capital project plans; in the next two months we are opening a health and wellbeing centre and we are also seeking to increase the proportion of disadvantaged pupils who attend our school.

The importance of single-sex schools

The best thing about a single-sex girls' education is that girls are completely free to make their own choices. In some schools, girls are the striking minority in maths and physics classes, perhaps because there are subconscious notions floating around about what a 'girl's subject' is. But, in a single-sex school, girls can be free of the notion that some subjects are not for them. (In Henrietta Barnett, for example, we have two huge and successful A-level physics sets: 95 girls doing maths A-level and 50 doing further maths.) Girls' schools enable more academic freedom and ambition, a real sense that there are no limits to what a girl can do. They can find their potential and flourish.

This translates more broadly. At Henrietta Barnett the pupils strongly believe in the power of women to do what they want. Dame Henrietta Barnett, our founder, was a pioneering woman, operating in the face of Victorian and Edwardian challenge and disapproval. Our pupils feel this. They know they are in a very special school founded by a very special woman. And whilst we still have a gender pay gap and women are still underrepresented in the top jobs in the FTSE 100, there is still a battle to be fought and won. Our students feel that they are part of that mission. Who knows, single-sex girls' schools may not be needed in 100 years' time… but right now, it feels that there is a powerful purpose we need to fulfil.

This is not just about addressing inequity in society, it's also about how girls and women see themselves and carry themselves confidently in mixed environments. We talk to them a lot about how they need to hold themselves and present themselves; how to be confident in speaking out, because they will absolutely need to have that self-assurance in mixed environments in the future. Most of our girls really recognise the value of a single-sex environment in their formative years.

Undoubtedly, for some, it is not usual to be educated in a single-sex environment and some of our pupils think that they are missing out by not being with boys; they feel that they are being deprived and that it will be weird when they get to university. But the reality, of course, is that when they get to university, they realise they haven't missed out on anything at all.

In addition, some girls might feel that an all-female environment is too intense: such a lot depends on the environment of the particular school. It is true that girls' friendship groups can be tricky to navigate and girls' schools have to work hard at that. Equally, for some pupils (as with any school anywhere) the environment won't be 100% right for them.

Still, most of our girls are relieved about not having to worry about what they look like at school; not having to wear mascara in Year 8. It is a genuine relief for them not to see a boy from dawn to dusk and, instead, to have a real sense of female camaraderie. The Girls' Day School Trust (GDST) produced a very interesting paper written by Kevin Stannard (2021), which showed that single-sex girls' schools still had a place. It was evidence-based and highly persuasive.

But not all schools should be single sex. One of the great things about the education system in the UK is the richness and variety on offer here. Parent choice is important just as it is important that students have choices. We have 3,000 pupils apply every year at 11+, so, whilst we recognise that globally it is unusual for girls and boys to be educated separately, it is very clear that people actively want the kind of education we are offering.

How is the school's ethos shaped by being single sex?

Interestingly, Henrietta Barnett did not set out to open a girls' school. She wanted to open a school in Hampstead Garden Suburb (which she founded, designed and built) and there were already some boys' schools around but not much on offer for girls, so she went ahead and opened a girls' school. So she wasn't particularly motivated about educating girls *per se*. But from the start, she wanted it to be 'a first class high school'. It was academically selective right from the beginning. She was determined for it to be the best, because everything she did had to be the best, and we remain proud custodians of that.

Perhaps you can see our single-sex status most clearly in educational terms in our focus on oracy. We are very concentrated on generating debate and discussion, on providing opportunities for girls to speak in class. We hold them to account on that in lessons. They have to come up to the board a lot; in maths and science, for example, they have to work problems through on the board. We require them to explain their thinking precisely and accurately to others. There is a lot of emphasis on debate. This is about a confident articulation of learning and ensuring that students are using appropriate technical terms and language; that we are generating a higher level of academic discussion. We want them to articulate and justify their ideas in depth, to really focus on their explanations. This is important pedagogically but, as referenced above, the need for women to own their spaces and find their voices means that this pedagogical approach is perhaps particularly significant for girls. We definitely recognise the need in some of our girls to develop more confidence in the way they articulate and present themselves. They are apt to be very polite and to express themselves too gently and we need to ensure, again, that as women they can be forthright and own the spaces they will be going into! Our parents tend to support this approach.

That emphasis on discussion is also an important part of pastoral education in our school. In PSHE (Personal, Social and Health Education), we have found it really beneficial to have single-sex environments in which to talk to girls about sex and relationships and drugs, etc. When the Everyone's Invited website landed, it was very good to be able to talk to girls on their own about those issues. That said, we were fortunate to be able to work with local boys' schools too and to have some joint discussions with boys on some of those matters.

We also think that there is a real benefit in being specialists in girls' education when it comes to identifying different kinds of neurodiversity, particularly given the fact that girls on the autistic spectrum or with ADHD (Attention Deficit Hyperactivity Disorder) can be very good at masking or modifying particular behaviours or characteristics which are more strikingly evident in autistic boys or those with ADHD.

In terms of our overall ethos and approach, we have very few rules. This is a very calm community and that is partly because it is single sex. And indeed, our relatively small site is relevant to who we are. We don't have the kind of space and grounds that Edwardian boys' schools would have had; all those pitches and playing fields… But our size is a strength in some ways – we 'hold' our pupils on top of the hill! We are a very friendly and warm community. That said, it is interesting that, historically, girls' schools often had to make do when it came to site or location. (Indeed, when Henrietta Barnett was established, it was designed to share space set aside for the adult education Institute in Hampstead Garden Suburb.) Is there an interesting correlation about the kind of space granted to girls historically in society and the fact that we now need to train them to take and fill their metaphorical and literal spaces with confidence?

Apart from those families with traditional values, who particularly appreciate the single-sex nature of our school, our parents are not strongly motivated by the fact that we are single sex. Our girls are ambitious, do well and go on to flourish at university and beyond. That's the greatest motivator for parents.

The future of single-sex schools

Henrietta Barnett is a beacon school in the UK and we are offering an outstanding education, so we don't feel any existential threat at the moment. But, unsurprisingly perhaps, funding is a huge issue for us. It is genuinely challenging to offer the quality education that we offer, on the current funding levels. We are punching above our weight, but our per-pupil funding for next year has gone up by 50p per pupil! That's it! And this is not just about not being able to offer the kind of facilities that private schools can offer. This is about teacher pay. How, with that level of increase, in an inflationary environment, can we fund competitive pay for teachers? How can we attract, recruit and retain really high-calibre teachers, without sufficient funds? It is really difficult and not getting any easier.

The question of single sex in the context of the recent significant recalibration of gender is, of course, important. We had already had some students identifying as male or non-binary and we have individuals now who don't identify as female. We are fine about this: we are a very relaxed school, and we are pleased that we are a warm and inclusive environment, such that our pupils feel able to come forward and let us know that they are identifying in a particular way – everyone at school is supportive. So, in that sense, it is straightforward. But there are connected issues. We are careful not to use the words 'girls' or 'women' too much.

The related issue here across education, is to do with the difficulties of articulating views that do not reflect the majority view. It is increasingly hard to do that, and I worry that there are some students who, if they have a view which is not in line with the majority, feel they have to keep quiet about it. But expressing our views is such a key part of the liberal tradition and of free speech. Increasingly though, it feels as though there is an accepted truth which may not be everyone's truth, but those who don't subscribe to it feel that they can't speak up and that is troubling.

In the end, though, what is most important is that everyone feels valued as an individual and that you can be who you want to be at school.

Another view

Counter-balancing the views put forward by the interviewees is the argument in favour of co-educational schooling given by Professor Lise Eliot. Here she puts an alternative view from the perspective of European and American education. There are also contributions from a number of heads of co-educational schools throughout the book in other chapters that might add to the debate.

Professor Lise Eliot, Professor of Neuroscience at the Stanson Toshok Center for Brain Function and Repair Chicago Medical School, Rosalind Franklin University

Single-sex schooling is as old as formal education, originating in the moral stance that boys and girls need to be prepared for different lives and equipped with different skills. It was only convenience – small, rural communities that lacked the resources for parallel classrooms – that prevented the separation of sexes in European and American education through most of history.

This changed in the 20th century, when feminists began challenging the lesser opportunities that gender-segregated education presented to girls. They worked hard to open doors to traditionally male spaces, including schools. Once they did, girls and women quickly proved their mettle, and now out-achieve males academically across primary, secondary and higher education (UNESCO, 2022).

Nonetheless, the tradition of single-sex education has remained strong in many locales, mostly because of the high quality of certain long-established, well-resourced schools. No one wants to dismantle a successful school. When they do, it is more often all-boys schools that have gone co-educational, both to promote equity and to double their pool of high-achieving applicants. As has long been recognised, girls elevate boys' achievement in the classroom (Hoxby, 2006).

So, single-sex schooling today is largely directed toward girls, with the aim of providing a protected space to develop their leadership and STEM skills. In fact, large-scale data do not bear this out – girls from single-sex schools are no more likely to be college STEM majors or to ascend to leadership and STEM professions than girls from equally elite co-educational schools (Hoffnung, 2011). Nonetheless, the 'STEM empowerment' myth is loudly touted by schools and parents, perhaps as cover for their more urgent, sadly regressive motive of protecting girls from boys in all ways.

It is true that all-female mathematics classes and student councils can be empowering for adolescent girls. Some girls experience less stereotype threat in single-sex schools. But such benefits are fading as girls are now equalling or exceeding boys' achievement in STEM subjects and ascending to leadership positions on co-educational campuses from primary to higher education. And a particular downside of empowerment in an all-female space is that it gives girls no opportunity to lead boys, or to prepare them more generally for mixed-sex relationships both in and outside the workplace. The 'real world' is co-ed, and it can be argued that developing healthy adult relationships and true gender equity requires a lot more, rather than fewer, opportunities for girls and boys to learn together, collaborate, compete and befriend each other during their formative years.

The same can be said about all-boys' schools, which are having something of a resurgence in low-resourced communities. In this case, however, academic achievement data are even less compelling (Pahlke et al, 2014) and it has proven difficult to create empowering all-male environments without simultaneously cultivating male supremacy.

To some, it seems bizarre that 21st-century leaders would even think about segregating pupils by gender. In many countries, segregating by religion or race or any other form of identity is not allowed, as most communities appreciate the importance of cultivating a diverse and tolerant citizenry. And given the growing numbers of children rejecting the gender binary, the idea of creating a sharp educational boundary between boys and girls seems especially regressive.

Reflections

What do girls' schools offer?

To what extent are girls' schools defined – and restrained – by their pasts? Originally created in opposition to the expectations society had of both sexes, interviewees suggest that girls' schools were thought of in terms of what they weren't, rather than what they were. Is this still true?

Loren Bridge continues to lead all strategy and operations in Australasia for ICGS. She attended both co-educational and single-sex schools, and has worked in both too. After working in corporate communications for over twenty years, she moved into education. Bridge's position is that societies around the world are making 'glacial' progress towards true equality (for example, in Australia the pay gap has remained around 15% for twenty years) 'girls have nothing to lose and everything to gain from a single-sex education'. Indeed, for her, the biases that are evident in almost every aspect of adult life are inevitably present in schools. When we interviewed her she said that 'the unconscious stereotyping and biases that often exist in co-educational schools – from teachers giving more attention to boys in classes and encouraging boys to do STEM subjects while directing girls to humanities subjects (Gentrup and Rjosk, 2018; Hofer, 2015; McCoy et al, 2021; Meland and Kaltvedt, 2019), to research showing that girls are less confident (Archard, 2012; AQR International, 2021; Fisher et al, 2015; Fitzsimmons et al,

2018; Fitzsimmons et al, 2021; Riggers-Piehl et al, 2018), and have lower self-esteem and body image issues (Cribb and Haase, 2016; Kim et al, 2018) – are simply not present in single-sex schools'.

Recent research by Doug Strycharczyk and Lia Zalums (2021), which argues that girls taught in single-sex schools tend to have more 'mental toughness' than those taught with boys, seems to support Bridge's claims. Bridge boldly states that 'single-sex schools may just be the answer to gender inequality'.

We live in highly visual times, where images are exchanged every second, and harmful stereotypes can be reinforced through old and new media. For proponents of girls' schools, being able to carve out 'safe spaces' is essential. As John Murphy argues, in a girls' school:

'A girl can comprehend her value and her capabilities in ways that have nothing to do with how she looks or how she is perceived by boys. She can be free to explore and try new opportunities, inside and outside of the classroom. She can follow her ambitions without wasting a second thought or a backward glance on how her male counterparts might perceive her.'

Perhaps the pandemic – which saw lessons move online and onscreen – exacerbated certain issues. The 'male gaze' may be absent in a girls-only school, but the pitiless scrutiny of high-resolution screens persuaded many young people to switch their cameras off. Provoking the question: is the constant self-scrutiny as our lives are increasingly lived out in public, and online, the most distracting of all?

Removing the glass ceiling

Jenny Brown, Head of City of London School for Girls, argues that the 'male gaze' may indeed be absent, but it is the male voice, and presence, which is most notably absent. Without boys, she further argues that 'some girls can vocalise in a different way. Also boys can take up more room. Such things affect how a school runs. Our pupils feel they own their place. They feel confident on an individual level and are politically active, resourceful and engaged.' And although she says that her school is proudly single-sex, she reports that the reality is that parents probably opt to send their daughters there not because boys are absent, but because 'of the exciting scholarly environment and the fact that they value the exciting co-curricular opportunities on offer'. The same is true for Henrietta Barnett School and for City of London School. They all feel that the parents choosing their schools are not doing so primarily because they are single-sex schools.

Megan Murphy is the Global Executive Director of ICGS, an organisation that represents girls' schools across the world, and she is passionately committed to the advancement of girls' education. Like Loren Bridge, she believes progress towards true equality is too slow and schools can help bridge the gender gap between the sexes: 'this deficit has resulted in women making up only 26% of employees in the UK's tech industries – a proportion unchanged for over ten years [(Tech Nation, 2021)].' To some extent, like Strycharczyk and Zalums's research, confidence plays a significant role in determining a girl's success. Murphy points to research by the ICGS which shows that graduates from girls' schools have higher levels of self-confidence in their ability to use technical science skills, understand scientific concepts, generate research questions, and to explain the results of a study (Riggers-Piehl et al., 2018).

Why might this be? For Murphy, 'it's because girls' schools have no glass ceilings. There are no assumptions about what girls like or prefer, because no one is telling them certain skills or subjects are "just for boys" or that they're too difficult to master. Everyone is held to the same expectations. And at girls' schools, younger students can see their older counterparts excelling in those same areas and subjects – allowing them to more easily develop the confidence to do the same.'

This modelling of achievement by older female students is clearly possible in a co-educational school, but it may be less self-evident and, possibly, more confined to certain subjects and activities. Murphy is adamant:

'Young girls need educational environments that allow them to break free from stereotypes to model leadership, innovation, agency, and self-efficacy. Because no matter what she wants to be when she grows up, a young girl needs to know – not just think, but truly know, deep down –she won't let anything stand in her way.' Or, to put it another way: 'a school *for* girls is better than a school *with* girls'. The quantity of opportunity is as important as the quality of the education provided: 'girls take centre stage, in everything. Girls occupy every seat in student government, every spot on the math team, and every position in the robotics club. By subtracting boys, an all-girls education adds opportunities for girls. That's because every aspect of a girls' school – from the classroom to the athletic field to the academic and extracurricular programs – is designed for girls.'

Is it possible to have a school *for* rather than simply *with* all young people?

What do boys' schools offer?

What sort of role model should boys' schools be offering to their pupils? How should these schools navigate perceptions which could, for some, seem at best archaic and limiting and, at worst, problematic and damaging? Research by the International Boys School Coalition (The Telegraph, 2010) suggests that educating boys should include activity and physical movement, hands-on learning, healthy competition and a competitive aspect to tasks and challenges, the element of surprise and unpredictability, and fun. But how distinctive are these requirements for any one group of pupils?

How have boys-only schools changed their aims and moved away from characteristics that were historically argued to be distinctively male? For Alan Bird:

'There is a much greater focus on looking after our mental, as well as our physical, health, and empathy for the simple truth that every pupil is likely to face their own challenges and insecurities: simply "toughing it out" is not a good approach to dealing with that. And, of course, celebrating the fact that boys, as well as girls, may flourish in the fields of art and music, as well as sport. Boys' schools can possibly engage with attempts to dismantle casual assumptions more easily, with their pupils freed from any need to perform to a gender stereotype in the presence of girls.'

The questions that come from such an approach are many, but perhaps the most obvious is: how can schools attempt to dismantle assumptions and stereotypes and provide persuasive, and complete, alternatives for their students?

Bradford Gioia references his school's motto: 'Gentleman. Scholar. Athlete' and, as Gioia points out, 'in that order'. For him, getting a boy to develop into being not just a man, but a gentleman, is the primary aim of the school he has led for 28 years. There is a focus on traits that the boy 'will hone throughout his life: empathy, resilience, honesty, courage, integrity, honour, humility'. He asks, 'It is a genuine challenge to get the boys to interact meaningfully with girls, but is that more important than finding out who they, the boys, really are?'

For Peter Broughton, Headteacher at Westminster City School, it's all about challenging the toxic stereotypes and powerful online messaging that is pervasively available for boys growing up today. He sums up the school's approach very neatly; they are seeking to move their boys from 'bravado to brave resilience'. Schools exist in different cultural and societal contexts – Gioia, for example, is speaking from a particular US context and Broughton from a particular UK context. But in all contexts, this is a significant challenge. Can – and how can – schools and school leaders seek to take on such a task?

The changing landscape for men and women

Alan Bird prefers to celebrate diversity, not masculinity. Bird sees his responsibility to the individuals who attend the school and does not define them purely according to their sex:

'Every one of [the boys] is an individual, with different interests, talents, challenges and ambitions. It is the responsibility of any school, single sex or co-educational, to cater to that heterogeneity, and to see diversity as something to celebrate. And alongside any crisis of masculinity, we also need to ensure that the boys don't leave school with any sense of entitlement based upon their sex. It requires a nuanced approach to language and pastoral care.'

As referenced earlier, according to Fortin et al (2013), in many societies it seems that women and girls are outperforming their male peers in almost every area of education. For Richard Reeves (quoted in Rabbitt, 2023), the liberation of women has been a welcome revolution, but it has created issues which many societies are still struggling to resolve:

'When my dad became unemployed, there was no question that his job was to get another job. There was a simplicity and clarity of male and female roles in those days. Of course, the problem was it was based on unjust inequality. But one of the advantages was that there was a very clear script for men and women.

Now, we have successfully rewritten the script for women in an expansive and empowering way: we've sent the message to girls and women that they can do anything. It's an incredibly liberating and expansive message that's broadened and enlarged the possibilities for women. In the space of a generation, we tore up the script for my mom (be a wife and mother) and wrote a new one for my wife (you go be an educational and economic equal!).

At the same time, we tore up the script my dad had (be the provider) but we forgot to re-write it. The result? Without a script, men must improvise their way to purpose, status, and security in the world. And improvising is hard, especially for those without skills, status, or economic resources. And that can lead boys and men to some really dark places as a result.'

But seeing progress in binary terms – with women forging ahead and men falling behind – is too simplistic. It ignores ethnicity and class (among many other factors). Other statistics complicate matters: for instance, in the interview with Henrietta Barnett School it was suggested that that the gender pay gap remains stubbornly wide. According to Reeves (2023), in the USA, for every \$100 men earn women earn \$82. Not all men are part of an elite, but not all men are failing; there are many affluent White middle-class boys and men who have better life chances than girls from disadvantaged backgrounds. And those life chances change depending on which country you focus on. In the United Kingdom, almost one million working-class children (mostly White boys) are faring worse in education than any other minority group except boys from the Gypsy, Roma and Traveller communities (Brassington, 2022). Only 16% of White children on free school meals go on to study at university, compared to 32% of Black Caribbean pupils, 59% Black African pupils and 73% Chinese pupils (DfE, 2021).

Understandably, we very often tend to focus on extremes in this area: much of the debate in many school systems is to see boys as failing and girls as succeeding.

But to see the progress of girls as a passage of unhindered joy is misguided. As the chapter on wellbeing shows, the mental health issues most closely associated with anxiety, depression and appearance are affecting young females more than any other group, and this appears to be cutting across all social groups, driven, it would seem, by the growing ubiquity of social media and mobile technology.

How does a single-sex school conform to changing societal norms?

Dividing children using any measure is inevitably going to be a blunt instrument. In her interview, Professor Lise Eliot describes single-sex education as a 'bizarre' act that is not replicated by using another aspect of one's identity in schooling. She argues that perhaps true equity can only be achieved by providing more opportunities for all young people to work closely together, rather than fewer. That is what the co-educational environment provides. So what might a single-sex educational environment offer?

Gioia quotes approvingly David Brooks' idea (Brooks, 2017) that some institutions are 'thick' and some are 'thin'. For Brooks 'thick institutions' exist physically, where people meet regularly. For the people who work in such a place, it can become inseparable from how they see themselves. They are places, ideally, where people meet at lunch, and which have idiosyncratic, distinctive identities. Schools fit such a profile. Brooks also suggests that individual cultures are important and that too many colleges feel like one another. And this, perhaps, goes to the heart of this chapter. Should a school be distinctive from other schools? If so, can a school remain distinctive, but also conform to (changing) societal norms and indeed how much should they conform?

Chapter 3

Traditional and progressive approaches to education

Schools often exhibit pride in their traditions. These traditions can provide a way of binding together pupils from different backgrounds. They may take the form of assemblies, proms, or prize-giving ceremonies at the end of the school year; each will have their own, unique provenance, their own special meaning to the school. And then, there are those implicit traditions that pass by mostly unnoticed, prosaically, every day: the names of rooms, or the routines that a school undertakes at certain times, the sports events, the year group names and the titles of the student leaders who head them up, the school uniforms and the rules that are liked or loathed in equal measure. Each, taken individually, might be inconsequential, but to suggest removing all of them together could be seen by the school community as undermining its core identity. In this sense, schools are places of tradition, but many school leaders would argue that they are not, by extension, traditional: to move from the noun to the adjective risks being characterised as opposed to change, to progression and to innovation. When it comes to schools, tradition and the traditional, as our interviewees might argue, are not the same thing at all.

Some of the interviewees in this chapter talk about 'fights' within education. It is perhaps no coincidence that the name of a well-known teaching blog in England is called *Scenes from the Battleground*. Some see 'trad' (traditional) teaching and 'prog' (progressive) teaching set out against one another. Those who align themselves, broadly, with traditional methods of teaching are likely to believe in a 'knowledge-rich curriculum', and the primacy of the teacher as *the* authority figure who imparts knowledge and is central to how pupils learn. High-stakes examinations, for traditionalists, are the fairest and most accurate form of assessments. Those who describe themselves as progressive see the teacher as only one source of information; they value 'child-centred learning' where the pupil has agency over their own education. Subjects are perhaps more likely to be interdisciplinary, and assessments, for a progressive teacher, may take many forms, including project-based work, portfolios and online, adaptive tests. This dichotomy between two ways of teaching, and two ways of running a school, means that school leaders might find themselves balancing what is acceptably progressive and what is forgivably traditional, as the interviewees discuss.

Take seating plans. You might think that how a teacher arranges pupils in the classroom is a relatively uncontroversial issue, but that may not necessarily be true. Educational consultant, author and former headteacher Tom Sherrington (2018) has written:

> 'Some of the strangest debates or memes about education that pop up now and then are about the idea of students sitting in rows. You don't have to look too far to find people aligning this commonplace desk configuration along the axis of evil. Only recently, I came across a tweet that mentioned children sitting in rows in a list of features of modern schooling that included [the words] compliant, submissive… It's just the weirdest thing. But it's not uncommon. Sitting rows = factory schooling, 19th C, Gradgrindian, "Victorian" – all intended as pejoratives.'

For many progressives, row after row of desks and chairs may be, as Sherrington states, a symbol of pedagogical rigidity. Traditionalists might argue back that they have continued with this arrangement because they think it works: they can see everyone's faces and make eye contact more easily when pupils sit in rows.

If seating plans are an unusually contentious area, so too is the (outwardly at least) benign issue of group work and collaborative learning (which is, of course, inseparable from how pupils are arranged together). For those who broadly subscribe to a traditionalist view of education, group work might be an unwanted distraction that allows pupils to veer 'off task'. Many others would argue that group work can lead to excellent work, and positively contribute to pupils' progress. Does child-centred learning work more effectively with more able children? It is not always easy to know because there are so many variables: what role does the teacher play? How important is the clarity of the tasks set? If the school is co-educational, should the groups be a mix of girls and boys? How does age change outcomes? Research conducted by the Education Endowment Foundation (no date) states:

> '… effective collaborative learning requires much more than just sitting pupils together and asking them to work in pairs or group; structured approaches with well-designed tasks lead to the greatest learning gains.'

Perhaps it is because many student teachers are taught about the Piagetian classroom (activity-based learning using a range of stimuli) and the Vygotskian approach (where active participation and collaboration are at the heart of assisted discovery learning) alongside teacher-led exposition, that the debate about what role the teacher should play in the classroom continues to be re-evaluated. How often are any of these philosophies openly challenged or questioned by those who teach aspiring teachers? What sense can busy teachers make of all this? Are a wide range of approaches promoted and explored without them being labelled as 'progressive' or 'traditional'? Is it possible for teachers and trainee teachers to focus on asking: 'Does it work in this school and for these pupils?'

As seen in the interviews in this chapter, many schools might seek to uphold their traditions, and at the same time, present themselves as modern, forward-looking and inclusive. The interviewees feel passionately that their traditions work well in their contexts, but teachers work with young people whose lives are, by their very nature, invested in the future. Does it therefore make sense to focus more exclusively on the future? Does rejecting the past risk valuing novelty? What value might traditions offer to schools, if any? The interviewees that we talk to in this chapter are acutely aware of the balances that need to be struck: move too fast and they lose what they and the parents feel should be preserved; move too slowly and they risk, at best, institutional stasis and, at worst, stagnation.

We asked our interviewees to discuss not only what a traditional education means to them, but also the biggest challenges they believe they face, and how they navigate the push and pull of modern society. Also explored is the way in which traditions may in fact complement more progressive approaches. It is worth noting that views put forward by some of the individual schools are quite strongly worded and therefore perhaps at odds with other educational perspectives. The 'Another view' feature, therefore, provides an alternative perspective to balance the discussion. The hope is that these interviews will promote reflection and debate.

Michaela Community School

Fact file

Number of pupils: 703

Age range: 11–18

Co-educational/Single sex: Co-educational

Location: UK

State-funded/Independent: State-funded

When was it established? 2014

Head/Contributor: Katharine Birbalsingh

Our pupils come from: The London borough of Brent. Ofsted commented that 'The proportion of pupils at the school who are disadvantaged is above the national average. The proportion of pupils who have special educational needs and/or disabilities is average.'

Our values: We aim high at Michaela Community School and expect high standards of behaviour and academic effort and achievement from all our pupils.

Our academic vision: We will enable our pupils to develop the habits of self-discipline. Pupils will appreciate that success needs hard work, however we also ensure that pupils who are struggling to keep up receive the help and support they need from our teachers to catch up.

Our pastoral vision: The goal is always that excellent behaviour and excellent learning should be second nature, not something that one has to work at constantly; it should simply be the way that we are. This is a state of mind that we want all our pupils to attain and sustain, not just at school, but for the rest of their lives.

What does a traditional education mean to you?

It means teaching in a traditional fashion. It means having teachers, with authority, at the front of the room, and in charge. It is teacher-centred teaching, as opposed to child-centred learning, which has children learning in groups. This is because the teacher knows more than the children and should be imparting knowledge, rather than being more of a facilitator of learning, who moves from group to group trying to keep the children on task.

It also means a traditional approach to discipline and accepting, again, that the teacher is in a position of authority, and it is for us to lead and shape the child in terms of his or her moral core, in understanding right from wrong. We would not just allow for an 'anything goes' approach, but instead have a clear *telos* ['purpose' or 'goal'] in mind for the child in terms of their moral and social development.

Creativity comes from knowledge and discipline. People like proxies, they like things to look a certain way. And they're not interested in the way things actually *are*. Tradition, knowledge, discipline, these inspire true creativity. Those who subscribe to a 'progressive' view of education could be accused of having a superficial sort of creativity that looks and feels good, but isn't real. It is true that the teachers have less autonomy here at Michaela than they do somewhere else. But I don't see that as a loss.

At Michaela we believe there is such a thing as great teaching. Our detractors disagree. They think that there are all different types of great teaching. I think there's one great way to do heart surgery. Now, of course, there's tinkering around the edges with heart surgery, too. And sometimes you will come across a special situation and you have to do something slightly differently. But I do think that there is a 'best' way of doing it. And so I don't see it as a loss to train everybody to be the best that they can be.

It's quite hard to imagine what we do, because what we do is so different. So, I'm very clear when people apply for a job here: we only ever have one candidate in at a time for an interview, we wouldn't have six candidates in at the same time. I have a conversation with them always at the start, where I say: today isn't just about us figuring out whether we want you, it's about you figuring out whether you want us.

I give them specifics to look out for when they're on their tour. And I ask them to put themselves in the shoes of the teachers and to imagine themselves doing similar sorts of things. I point out the things they will no longer be able to do: for example, create lots of slideshows, decide what they want to do in their lessons... I point out that loss of autonomy, and I ask if they want that. I'm really explicit about it so that they're clear. Because what we do is very different.

Some parents find it very frustrating. We're not an independent school, so people don't necessarily choose us. Some people do and love us. But a number of our kids haven't actually chosen us, they are just given to us by the council. So, some of those parents will find it very frustrating, but they don't really have much choice, because there isn't necessarily anywhere else to go without a long wait and lots of trouble. What can also happen is that the kids are sent here, and then a waiting list place turns up at another school, after six weeks, or even six months, and the parent tells us they want to take their child out of Michaela and send them to that other school. Very often the child will say that they are happy with us and want to stay. I always say to schools, don't worry about the parents. You need to get the child on board with what you do.

Some parents find us frustrating because we insist on traditional things, like homework being done and their child being here on time. And we don't let up, we are relentless. But my duty is to the child, not to their parents, and in the end, their children end up with some great GCSEs and good characters.

The staff find that we work very hard; they give a lot, but they find it very rewarding. Perhaps in other places staff will work hard but not see the results of that hard work, but here it's immediate. They also love it because the good behaviour means that they can have amazing relationships with the kids. We have better relationships with our pupils because good behaviour is a given: you're not having to argue with the kids all the time, or force them to do stuff. They're just polite, lovely, kind individuals.

Because that's the expectation, the staff really love it. They love the project of trying to show the world what is possible. We get 800 guests a year, every year. They are all teachers from around the world. And what they always say is: this is unbelievable! I've never seen anything like it. How is this possible? How do you get kids to do this? And it is kind of mind-blowing when you see it. Because of my role, I hardly see any lessons, but when I do see them, I am also blown away. I always think: 'This is amazing!' I get it. I have the experiences of the guests myself.

And the kids are so grateful. They're just thrilled to be in a school where they're learning so much. And they know the difference between them and their friends at other schools. They feel really clever and really successful. They change as people, and their parents recognise this as well; they know that their kids are working harder than ever. They don't have to tell them to get on with their homework. The kids are nicer people at home, they're thanking their families for making them dinner and looking after them.

What are the biggest challenges you face?

It's the culture wars, and you're fighting this fight with people who insist there is no fight happening. I have to remember the *telos*: to give kids an excellent education, not just within this building, but in the country, to influence people who know deep in their hearts that there is something wrong, and who know they're looking for something better.

And I run into people like this all the time on the street, who come up to me and say: 'I used to think you were a bit mad, but I've been following what you do for a couple of years and I now realise that what you say makes sense'. And those people, those quiet people who cannot speak out, I'm doing it for them, I'm doing it for those children who do not have a voice, but who want an education. I think we've got used to teaching a way of being that is not necessarily conducive to the success of all children.

We all learn best when being taught traditionally: being told stuff by the teacher. That doesn't mean all you do is rote learn. About 10% is rote learning. What is quite sad is that what is represented as a 'traditional classroom' in some debates is a caricature, created by those who oppose such things. That is regrettable because so many people who could have been great teachers have been stopped from being so because they think, misguidedly, that they will be letting the children down if they teach in a traditional way. The culture wars have their roots in this initial, progressive movement of child-centred learning, in allowing the child to decide what's best for him or her, as opposed to the adult being in the position of authority. We've all lost sight of what is true, but we have to keep fighting. All of us. We have to keep fighting for what's right and true.

To what extent are the pressures of a modern society at odds with a school that promotes tradition?

It's exhausting. I'm like a professional fighter! I'm just constantly fighting everybody. And I'm saying things that seem to be common sense as far as I'm concerned. It feels like the rest of the world has gone mad. For example, we're currently planning to take some kids to a well-known bookshop in London. And one of my teachers organising it had to check the children's section out in advance, and he found books that were simply not appropriate for young children.

Sydney Grammar School

Fact file

Number of pupils: 1,970

Age range: 5–18

Co-educational/Single sex: Single sex (boys' school)

Location: Australia

State-funded/Independent: Independent

When was it established? 1854

Head/Contributor: Dr Richard B Malpass

Our pupils come from: All parts of the greater Sydney area, taking in boys of all different socio-economic backgrounds given our centrality in the heart of the Central Business District of Sydney with public transport links to most parts of the wider Sydney area.

Our values: Intrinsically linked to an explicitly academic education for its own sake. We believe that young people prosper when their academic subjects, their sports, their music, their arts and so forth are pursued for their own essential beauty and validity. Herein, we draw quietly on the Newtonian notion of 'standing on the shoulders of giants', in that our boys become increasingly aware of the wondrous enormity of thought, debate and achievement which has preceded their time at the school.

Our academic vision: Broadly to sustain and develop a series of campuses in which learning, academic enquiry and ultimately achievement are entirely natural and genuinely unadulterated ambitions. Whilst we respect the need to make our boys 'job ready', we value the richer depths of learning which don't necessarily announce themselves as relevant to employment readiness. Ultimately, this is because we believe that a genuinely powerful and rounded academic education will equip our boys for a life of intellectual enthusiasm and dedication which will trailblaze far beyond the acquisition of their first jobs in the workforce. The school will have done its best work for each boy if he leaves the school as a rocket leaves a launch pad. Let him peak well above the stratosphere of his personal expectations.

Our pastoral vision: Intimately associated with our academic aims and ambitions. Our house and tutor systems are well-established and designed to ensure that we know our boys well and that they and their parents feel that there is a close and caring blanket of support throughout their time at the school.

What does a traditional education mean to you?

From our earliest days, Sydney Grammar School prioritised a purity of academic purpose above what today might be called 'relevant job readiness' in the hope of creating widely read and inspired thinkers. Given the inevitably changing nature of what will be considered professions in the years to come, it will be very important for our young men to have a pure academic grounding in order to be in a position to choose their path in the future. Thus, we remain true to our trustees' historic vision, and indeed, with practical, contemporary purpose.

One aspect of Sydney Grammar School is its insistence on classrooms in which technology is kept to a minimum unless a subject teacher specifically wants to make use of a particular device or application. It is fundamental to the school to engage the boys in debate, discussion and eye-to-eye dialogue, both in the classroom and around the grounds in their spare time. Thus, we have entirely resisted a move to devices in classrooms. We have a traditional approach to our boys' learning; a traditional pen-on-paper approach to the acquisition of knowledge, which is a powerful antidote to the screen-time trend of many schools. Of course, in today's technology-reliant world, learning how to effectively learn and work with technology is an absolute necessity. Certainly, proficiency in an age of ubiquitous devices is essential, and perhaps inevitable, regardless of the approaches adopted in the school classroom.

Nonetheless, it seems that those two discrete elements (the ubiquity of devices and the life of the classroom) have increasingly been merged in the forward thinking of so many educational leaders. A somewhat convenient logic has asserted that the existence of unprecedented technological possibilities will, *ipso facto*, transform the classroom to achieve unprecedented teaching and learning. This aspirationally crafted and technologically progressive 'classroom' is unsurprisingly termed the '21st-century classroom' by many, and its potential is frequently projected as so impressive as to dwarf the relatively limited classrooms of former eras, bereft (as they might now be seen) of our access to instantaneous online information and effortlessly interconnected approaches to work, general communication and limitlessly fascinating diversions. Consequently, discussions in the field of education in recent years are tightly linked to the role to be played by laptops, iPads® and BYODs (bring your own devices) in that envisaged classroom.

We should guard against the risk of losing focus on the essential qualities of a great classroom (whatever the century), and the core dynamic between a fine teacher and his or her students. It has been often said that students don't in every case easily 'learn subjects' but that in so many cases they 'learn teachers', a seemingly flippant but often highly relevant reflection of the primacy of the teacher's too frequently underestimated role as the inspirer and engager of the young people in their classroom.

Over the years, I've been privileged to witness and learn from a very wide range of teachers across five major schools in Australia and the UK. As an observer of so very many lessons delivered by other teachers, it has become abundantly clear that the most effective lessons were those in which the teacher's presence, his or her subject knowledge, that palpable passion and communicative warmth in sharing the experience of their topic, simply inspired the room.

By contrast, there seems to be a trend in some recent thinking about pedagogy that the teacher should take something of a backward step and largely cease to be the focus of the lesson; rather, he or she should be a facilitator. The focus should move to 'student-centred' learning, a branding that seemingly presumes to dismiss other classrooms as monolithic chalk and talk. By contrast, I would argue that true student-centred learning is at its peak when a child is shielded from distractions and utterly focused on the idea-rich classroom that such an engaging teacher has brought to academic life. Thus, I do not think that such student-centric learning can best come through the teacher being limited to a facilitator who takes a back seat to the laptop, simply alerting those students to relevant websites and setting them projects to pursue.

One of the chief delights of being involved with the life of Sydney Grammar boys is to witness, and be part of, their inexhaustible thirst for discussion and debate, perhaps the key facet of our collective intellectual life. The opportunities for exciting learning through various computer and device-based approaches will continue to evolve and be adopted by Sydney Grammar Masters (teachers) as they see appropriate. Thinking teleologically, we should remind ourselves that laptops, iPads® and the like were not necessarily designed to further the profession of education. There may well be an intersection between their various offerings and the best of educational practice, but the craft of our Masters and their classrooms, together with their exciting Socratic dimensions, have more than a little life in them yet.

What are the biggest challenges you face?

Parents sometimes need to be reminded that we value the traditional methods of teaching and learning compared to technology-based learning, as they remain powerfully successful.

Our approach allows our Masters to be the academic champions of their classrooms. Although they can deploy whatever devices and applications they choose (and we support whatever they suggest), the classroom experience remains primarily an effusive interaction between an intellectual 'master' and his/her academically aspiring apprentices.

The relative absence of devices has been marvellous from a pastoral care perspective. Back in 2017 we observed at a sports day that far too many boys were spending their down-time between events on their phones with very little personal interaction. Shortly afterwards we announced that phones would be only accessible outside of school time. The response from parents was glaringly positive. Amongst the boys, handball became even more prolific, general friendly chatter even more abundant, and (joyously) books increased their prevalence around the place. Some boys grumbled, but at least they grumbled face to face to boys sitting next to them in the playground!

To what extent are the pressures of a modern society at odds with a school that promotes tradition?

I think that the uncomfortable and problematic disjunction between modernity and tradition is at a slightly worrying stage of late. In saying so, I am writing from a somewhat uniquely Australian perspective, as our curricula are undergoing review to assess the balance they might strike between academic demands and vocational 'relevance'. I would contend that the dichotomy between modernity and tradition is not so out of keeping with a similar dichotomy between academic ambitions and vocational relevance. The key dichotomy lies in the distinction between experiencing pure learning, literature, science, art and beauty ('academic') which should be handed down from generation to generation ('tradition') and the contrasting demand for vocational pathways from schools ('relevance') to justify the value of teaching a subject in job-outcome terms. At Sydney Grammar, we focus on the tradition of learning big ideas and allow the boys time later to worry about jobs, which they usually successfully achieve.

Royal Hospital School

Fact file

Number of pupils: 700

Age range: 11–18

Co-educational/Single sex: Co-educational

Location: UK

State-funded/Independent: Independent

When was it established? 1712

Head/Contributor: Mr Simon Lockyer

Our pupils come from: Pupils join Royal Hospital School (RHS) from all over the world including many from families serving in the armed forces (Army, Navy, Marines and RAF).

Our values: The traditional values of loyalty, commitment, courage, respect, service and integrity have underpinned the school's philosophy from the very beginning; 300 years later, they are as relevant to the education we provide now as they were then. Our mission is 'to understand each young person's strengths, to help them to make the right choices at the right time, navigating through their critical formative years and ensuring their education becomes the foundation for their happiness and success'.

Our academic vision: To develop intellectual curiosity and academic confidence in our pupils such that they fulfil their potential in all their endeavours and develop the ability to think and act creatively and imaginatively.

Our pastoral vision: To develop pupils who are adaptable, resilient and equipped to live healthy and fulfilling lives after school; who will uphold the school's unique and rich heritage and contribute to the life of the school and their community, and will embrace a global outlook with a respect for individuality and difference.

What does a traditional education mean to you?

I don't think it means a great deal as it implies to me an old-fashioned approach that is short on innovation and limited in its capacity to explore change. RHS provides an education that places equal value to the lessons and experiences that young people receive outside of the classroom. An education that is underpinned by values and an ambition to develop the whole person and to bolster self-belief has been a constant at RHS but feels particularly relevant for today's pupils and parents. Holding on to some of the traditions that are distinctive to RHS is important to current and former pupils and families and provides a shared common experience. For RHS, this takes the form of the traditions associated with our naval heritage but, rather than see these as historic traditions, we are keen that we focus on their value and relevance in developing skills and values.

Some pupils may naturally favour the non-academic and therefore academic attainment is not the be all and end all for pupils or the school. The school has seen consistent academic improvement, but accepting pupils may have strengths that are not acknowledged through formal assessment ultimately means that the pursuit of league table performance is a conscious decision. A traditional education certainly does not suggest that RHS cannot be progressive, innovative or experimental; our use of technology is just one example where we have, for some time, been in the vanguard and have not been afraid to try new technologies, knowing we can always change our approach.

What are the biggest challenges you face?

There is sometimes a conflict between perception – or reputation – and reality. In terms of tradition, there is no doubt that our maritime heritage and some of the associated traditions, such as the wearing of naval uniforms on a small number of occasions each year, leads to a very exaggerated reputation. Even regionally, the school is often referred to as 'the marching school' despite the fact that pupils have not marched around the school site for many years! The associations with the Royal Navy also cast a shadow that the school is focused on discipline, order and is preparing its pupils for life on the open sea. These stereotypes are incredibly outdated and far from the reality, but perception and reputation take a long time to counter, particularly when we hold onto, in a small way, some of the traditions.

Our traditions, that are largely linked to the routines within the calendar, have no influence on teaching and learning. The curriculum is designed to provide choice and breadth to meet the broad needs of the pupil demographic. As such, we have adopted a range of different courses alongside GCSE and A Levels which require different approaches in teaching and learning. Technology is very well-resourced and encourages staff and pupils to develop new approaches.

We do not allow traditional approaches to education to influence what we do today. To do so would be to confine our school to a fixed period in time and to hinder development, evolution and improvement.

RHS retains a very strong boarding ethos with a full weekend programme, and therefore pastoral care is essential. Alongside the fundamental structures needed to run a boarding school, we have had to constantly reassess the provision to meet the needs of the pupils and staff, with a far greater emphasis on creating balance, flattening traditional hierarchies and providing more opportunities for genuine dialogue between pupils and staff. The school community is incredibly diverse, and therefore enabling and promoting an understanding of difference has been a significant focus in recent years.

Parents want to see schools evolve and improve. Our parents value some of the traditions, but they would certainly not want our progress to be hindered by traditional approaches just because they are part of the way things have been done. It is often played back that RHS is a school that you do not really understand until you are part of it. What has struck me is that the parents are incredibly loyal and proud to be part of something that holds onto some traditions. It is probably somewhat self-selecting, but the emphasis on service and community are regularly acknowledged by parents and guardians as defining and special features of the school.

To what extent are the pressures of a modern society at odds with a school that promotes tradition?

A society that can often stress the importance of individuality and self can sometimes feel at odds with a school that places such an emphasis on community, teamwork, collaboration and service to one another. However, I do feel that, regardless of whether pupils are day or boarding, they quickly come to value the benefits of being part of something that is a constant, to be part of occasions and traditions that have endured for centuries and connect them with former pupils. There is little doubt that the vast majority of pupils develop a huge sense of pride in being part of Divisions (the school's ceremonial parades). Being part of a traditional boarding school community, regardless of whether they are boarding, creates some very strong shared experiences and therefore friendships. Being part of a community that is diverse also naturally helps to promote and celebrate difference rather than point to division.

Bedford Free School

Fact file

Number of pupils: 507

Age range: 11–16

Co-educational/Single sex: Co-educational

Location: UK

State-funded/Independent: State-funded

When was it established? 2012

Head/Contributor: Mrs Jane Herron

Our pupils come from: 60% of our pupils come from Bedford. Pupils who are admitted by distance from the school (rather than EHCP, LAC, sibling connection, etc.) live less than 1 km from the school which lies in the Cauldwell

Ward of Bedford. 28% of pupils receive pupil premium funding and there are in excess of 40 varying ethnicities amongst the school pupil population.

Our values: Respect, honesty and high expectations.

Our academic and pastoral vision: We believe that, given the right circumstances, all children are capable of extraordinary things.

In the future: We want to ensure that our progress 8 score is always 1 or above. We strive for every pupil to gain above 4 in all of their GCSEs. We would like a bigger and better site with room for more pupils (we are very oversubscribed; there are approximately four applications for every place) and playing fields (our school sits on one of the busiest roundabouts in Bedford town). We would love to provide a sixth form.

What does a traditional education mean to you?

I don't actually think that Bedford Free School provides a 'traditional' form of education. I actually think we're progressive. Of course, some people might say that it is traditional, but if I think of a traditional school, I see rows of individual desks with a strict, aloof teacher at the front, kids listening to the teacher lecturing non-stop in a monotone voice, or taking notes as the teacher writes on the board. That's certainly not what we're about.

However, we do regard the teacher as the subject expert and the teacher as the most important person in the room; it is the teacher who needs to be listened to. And we do expect the children to behave and remain focused, in order to learn. In the 1990s, right through to the 2010s, education became so progressive (involving group work, discovery-based learning, learning styles, building learning power, etc.) that you can see why, when people visit our school, they might view us as more traditional. In some respects, we've consciously gone back to a traditional education.

We are actually doing lots of new stuff, based on robust and deep research, for example in cognitive science or through the work of educationalists such as Christine Counsell, Daniel Willingham, Dylan Wiliam and Doug Lemov. We use such research to find the commonalities between great teachers, to share good practice. Being described as a traditional school might put some people off us: we might be, wrongly, viewed as draconian, or strict, and that would be a misunderstanding of who we actually are.

What we do is in the interests of the children. We don't allow mobile phones to be seen or heard and there are silent corridors. Feeling safe, getting from class to class without wasting a moment; such things count, they have an impact on learning. Our building is on five storeys which makes for incredibly echoey staircases. Having silent corridors helps to diminish sensory overload which supports neurodiverse pupils.

And we're oversubscribed. Some families who don't know us may worry about how we enforce rules, structure and routines but, in the long run, the children benefit. When you see pupils on results day gaining their grades, it's joyful. We record those moments and share them with younger children and their families, and they see this success and say that they understand why Bedford Free School is set up in the way it is.

Expectations are high. In class, in order to support focus, we encourage the children to look at the point of focus, which of course is most often the teacher; they must not talk in class unless they are invited to do so. We say 'track me', and they must then look at the speaker or the board, for example. We pay forward [prepare ahead] whenever we can. This means that, before their next lesson, the pupils take out all the equipment they need; they have to get ready to move on to the next lesson so they may start it immediately in a meaningful, purposeful way. In that sense, it is a traditional education (we don't insist you have to teach in rows although most of our teachers choose to do so for practical reasons, such as optimal eyes on pupils and vice-versa). We follow Lemov's idea of ratio [see Lemov, 2015]: we explicitly work on expecting a high participation and think ratio, and we use praise and narrating the positive to help us achieve 100% of pupils actively involved in their learning. We don't reprimand teachers who don't achieve this, but if you have a high number actively thinking then you are going to get a high proportion of students learning. These are challenges that we face every day; we work hard to sweat the detail and make the routines and expectations automated and part of 'who we are'.

Reading lots is also at the core of our school ethos. As well as encouraging as much reading in lessons as possible, for 30 minutes in the middle of every day our students have DEAR (drop everything and read). This is carried out as a whole tutor group, with everyone having a turn to read out loud and the tutor 'controlling the action'. At the end of most days, each student returns to their tutor for a third time where they carry out their prep (homework) in silence. All this is done with their tutors, who get to know them very well as they spend about 1 hour and 40 minutes daily in all with them. For one session a week, there is a 'tutor time' when the student and tutor look at rewards and attendance, and new weekly achievement cards are issued. These support a reward system that recognises those pupils who consistently work hard, are properly dressed, have all of their equipment and diligently carry out their homework.

What are the biggest challenges you face?

One of the biggest challenges a school like ours faces is that we risk being unpopular. But I'm not here to be loved. I want to be respected, and liked, but not for my personal benefit – because of the impact we've had on the children who attend the school. We talk about the variety of schools in and across sectors, but there is much that we have in common with all schools. Of course, we all want the best for the children in our care, for them to be happy, safe and educationally thriving and progressing. A headmaster of a local private school was very complimentary when he visited recently and commented on how familiar our routines are across lessons, the language used. There is a consistency across our school, but it is a challenge to maintain those high standards every day. We have to keep going back to ensure there is no drift in behaviour, reboot our expectations if standards have slipped, remind ourselves of what we want and the rationale for it, and work collaboratively with the teachers on how we can get back to where we want to be. Those are the daily challenges schools face.

The biggest challenge is our building. We need to grow. We need more space, we need a sixth form. We've exhausted all options. We are built on a roundabout in the middle of town. We had to fight for that! So perhaps the challenge is political, and whether such decisions at a local level – on planning for example – are influenced by our perceived traditionalism, we will never know. But free schools were a Conservative government initiative and I think that, sometimes, if you're dealing with a local council that is not Conservative-led, you have to be aware of that. But we won't give up because what we do is for our children. They deserve the best and that's what we'll fight for.

To what extent are the pressures of a modern society at odds with a school that promotes tradition?

When we first opened we used to say that we were 'a grammar school for all'. Bedford used to have four private schools (it now has three), and it seemed unfair that those parents in Bedford who could not afford those schools did not have access to an excellent education. When we opened, we wanted to offer as much as we could to those parents, to emulate some aspects of those private schools: private study, great enrichment opportunities and a focus on getting high grades. Much of what we offer is aimed at students receiving pupil premium funding, as well as vulnerable students; for example, our focus on quality-first lessons, clubs on the timetable, free after school intervention sessions and offering supported prep sessions (because pupils may not have the space at home to work or are not encouraged to do their homework).

And parents buy into us. Many put us down as their first choice (there are about ten mainstream schools serving the town). And they're delighted if they secure a place for their child. There is some pushback – about 5% – from parents when they realise that we do what we say we do in terms of our rules and expectations. But, overall, our parents are happy with us: for example, we usually get over 90%

turnout for progress evenings and very positive returns in parent surveys. And we encourage our parents to tour during the day to see us in action. It helps them to understand and feel aligned with our values, our approach.

The same goes for staff. Like our parents, we have to know that they buy into us, into our approach. Young teachers in particular can be idealistic and maybe want to compromise on some of the things we offer/do. They don't appreciate for example that some pupils need to be taught to behave or have aspiration instilled and that can cause problems. It is our job to keep communicating the 'why' in our approach to them and the pupils and their families. But we have a very high ratio of trainee teachers who want to return to us to work here full-time. They get it. They know that everything we do, we do for a reason. And I think the staff are secretly proud of it.

You need a lot of knowledge to be creative. We say to our students: Why would you not want to learn loads? And for you to learn, you have to be focused, you have to be silent, you have to be able to hear the teacher. But there is a significant part of society that simply refuses to understand such an approach. I find that frustrating. Perhaps such critics come from backgrounds where they have been privy as a child to being read to daily, being supported to do their homework, being surrounded by books... Or where there are regular family discussions over dinner about important issues. It is those sort of people who take for granted their privileges, who frequently criticise us, and similar schools, for being strict. But they are talking from a position of ignorance. They should visit schools where behaviour is not as good as here and then think about what we achieve. We are not selective; we are situated in the poorest ward in Bedford – about 30% of our children receive pupil premium funding. We are very ethnically diverse, with about 60 languages spoken. We're proud of what we achieve every day.

Harrow International School Hong Kong

Fact file

Number of pupils: 1,573

Age range: 3–18

Co-educational/Single sex: Co-educational

Location: Hong Kong

State-funded/Independent: Independent

When was it established? 2012

Head/Contributor: Tom Hicks (Principal Deputy Headteacher)

Our pupils come from: Hong Kong, China, overseas.

Our values: Honour, humility, courage, fellowship. Our global citizenship statement is: 'We are global citizens who recognise the diversity of the world and are aware of our place in it. We take leadership roles in our local and global communities, working collaboratively to create a kinder, more peaceful and sustainable world.'

Our academic vision: 'Educational excellence for life and leadership.'

Our pastoral vision: 'A caring, respectful community in which everyone thrives.'

In the future: We aim to continue to be the first-choice school in Hong Kong, a leading school in Asia and one of the top 100 schools in the world. Having been named by *Spear's Index* as one of the top 100 in the past three years, we feel in a good position to build on that platform, especially now COVID-19 restrictions have finally been dropped in Hong Kong.

What does a traditional education mean to you?

For us, it means a broad and balanced British curriculum in an Asian setting. We derive much of our tradition from Harrow School in London and yet, as a through-school with a 50/50 mix of girls and boys in a totally different cultural context, we are proud of our ten-year history and our own identity. We are pretty traditional in terms of offering GCSE and A level, but have the flexibility to adapt our curriculum outside the examined groups.

It's about fusing traditional independent school British tradition, with the modern Hong Kong international context. The Harrow values of honour, humility, courage and fellowship are timeless, but we do constantly reflect on what they mean for us in all aspects of school life. It can be quite incongruous seeing the traditional Harrow Hats being worn on a hot day at Remembrance for instance, but the pupils tend to embrace the traditions and make them their own. We also run the traditional Long Ducker race (held between Marble Arch and Harrow School in London) but we do it on the stunning MacLehose Trail behind our school and follow it with an international food and charity fair.

What are the biggest challenges you face?

Much the same as other schools: in the short-term, resetting expectations of behaviour post-COVID-19, and also delivering a curriculum which is appropriate in a world where AI and other technologies are challenging existing pedagogy. In many ways, keeping sight of the core values of education have never been more important: ensuring young people feel a sense of belonging, a recognition that they are part of something bigger than themselves, that their actions have impact and that they ought to act with moral purpose. At Harrow Hong Kong, our pupils have a great chance to be responsible and proactive global citizens and we hope to help them deliver on that responsibility.

Sometimes it can be challenging to make sure all stakeholders recognise that examination results are not mutually exclusive to a holistic approach. This is perhaps exacerbated a little in Hong Kong where the academic pressures are enormous and the private tutoring culture is ubiquitous, but I have seen this in the UK as well. The demand for university places does not seem to be abating and this leads to us needing to be very much on the front foot as far as pastoral support is concerned. This brings its own challenges in terms of myth-busting and addressing taboo subjects like mental health.

To what extent are the pressures of a modern society at odds with a school that promotes tradition?

The more the so-called modern world develops, the more the need for solid foundations on which our young people can rely as a moral bedrock. In uncertain times, coming back to a clear set of values can help ensure young people make decisions in a considered and consistent way, and are not necessarily swayed by popularism or external influences. As long as 'tradition' is not code for negative behaviours, it should be fostered. We are lucky that, with such a young school, you can really explore what your values and traditions mean, and there is scope for new ones.

Another view

In the following section, Alistair McConville puts forward a point of view diametrically opposed to the views put forward by our contributors, creating an interesting dynamic in the overall discussion about traditional and progressive education.

Alistair McConville, Deputy Head at King Alfred School, Co-founder of Rethinking Assessment and of the School Directed Courses Consortium.

Arguments from tradition belong with phrenology and leeches. 'Tradition' as justification should be viewed as a desperate recourse.

Any 'traditional' practice needs to be critically evaluated in the light of contemporary knowledge and changing societal contexts and priorities. Some may conceivably turn out to stand the test of time, but if they do, it will not be because they are 'traditional' per se, but because they remain relevant and effective in a different climate, are borne out by modern critiques and no better alternative method of achieving the same end has yet been found. Few traditions stand this test.

Arguments from tradition can be positively harmful. When applied to curriculum, they alienate some people for whom supposed social capital differs from their own values and heritage. They perpetuate cultural elitism and reinforce a nonsense that there is some sort of timeless 'Britishness' in which it is desirable to participate; which implies knowledge of particular texts and historical vignettes; where loyalty to inherited authority is somehow a virtue. Worst of all, they perpetuate disadvantage, since those most embedded in our socio-cultural hierarchies find themselves with a glaring head start.

The same goes for 'traditional' teaching and assessment methods. It is an absurdity that in the era of AI we continue to peddle a glut of summer tests with pen and paper, governed by unsmiling invigilators and a ticking clock, as the primary arbiters of intelligence and capability. Students tell us this process is excessively stressful and detracts from their love of learning; employers tell us it is not delivering the skills they need; universities deploy far more diverse methodologies to judge competence, leaving our regurgitation junkies unprepared and uninspired; other countries peer confusedly at our one-eyed exam obsession.

But 'exams are the best and fairest way of showing what young people know and can do' goes the traditionalist's mantra. This holds no water. Exam grading is stunningly unreliable in most subjects; they hover briefly over only a fraction of what students have learned and demand a single mode of expressing it, when many equally good ones exist. The bell curve dooms a third to fail before they pick up a pen and it is as easy to perpetuate your own advantage in the exam system as it is to cheat in coursework: get yourself a private tutor, buy yourself a place in a private school where small class sizes mean more individualised coaching for the test, pay for a review of marking until you like the outcome.

We need new ideas and tools for crediting our children for their varied strengths and interests, not a doubling down on 'tradition'. Digital learner profiles [an online student portfolio documenting an individual's qualifications and achievements], which encompass a variety of metrics, are a promising antidote to curriculum and assessment narrowness. Countries such as Australia are beginning to adopt them as a more subtle and broad representation of achievement. In a world increasingly aware of the benefits of all kinds of diversity, we need to provide a means to showcase its expression.

We are in thrall to an ideology of educational traditionalism sustained by a tiny number of social conservatives who have succeeded in turning back the clock. Their way risks the 'silent endurance' of *Tom Brown's School Days*. Joyless, noiseless corridors and pointless detentions. This approach is infantilising and retrograde, it fails to prepare our young people adequately and it blights their youth.

We must change with the times.

Reflections

Can the traditional be promoted in a modern society?

Should schools reflect the trends that are prevalent in a society? Should they promote shifting values, even if they sit uncomfortably with the teachers who are asked to do so? Should tradition be preserved at all cost, or should some aspects of the past be modified, or disposed of, to meet the expectations of the school's key stakeholders? What happens when the priorities of the school are in conflict with the values of parents? Perhaps those schools, like Sydney Grammar, that are unashamedly traditional in their approach to certain aspects of the modern world will be more secure in how they approach other complex areas, or perhaps not.

The interviews in this chapter suggest that there is a tension between the traditional and tradition: the former has associations of stasis, the latter with outward, physical shows of ingrained routine. The latter is often uncontroversial: Royal Hospital School is keen to preserve certain aspects of its naval past because they feel that it adds to the shared sense of self that is so important to the school. They state that the traditions do not threaten perceived progress in other areas (such as pastoral care or teaching). Tradition, then, is safe if, like a stone in a river, it allows change to move around it.

But to extend that simile a little: what if, over time, the water wins and the current of change wears away the stones of tradition, until the foundations themselves are dissolved? If traditional forms of knowing – and knowing oneself – are challenged and disputed, is this to the advantage or disadvantage of pupils? Disposing of tradition can become self-perpetuating. Out with the old, in with the new! And, for some, the past may be less glamorous than the present and arguably less exciting than the future. Alistair McConville's position is clear: we need to hurry this process along or risk failing the young people we teach.

The schools we talked to are both fee-paying and state-funded. Some are old, some new. But it is not these factors that seem to influence their attitude to tradition or the traditional. Our interviewees suggested that what does matter is the attitude of the school leaders: what they prioritise and promote crystallises the school's relationship with its past and the future it wants to create. They suggest that we make our own traditions; they are formed, and re-formed in the present, like a coastal shelf. They grow, layer on layer, with each successive generation of pupils who live them. Interviewees suggested that traditions can only survive with understanding and with a sincere appreciation of their meaning. If tradition and the traditional become performative, both in action and thinking, then they may soon become meaningless. Schools, like the human brain, can be repositories for memory. Joseph Jebelli observed in the book *How the Mind Changed* (cited in Robinson, 2023a), that the brain *is* memories, and this distinguishes it from even the most sophisticated computer program. Like the brain, a school is a complex collection of memories and experiences, many shared, even more known only to the individual. Those in schools are required to make sense of a huge amount of information. Is this only possible if there is an explicit commonality of behaviour and of understanding based on various areas of shared experience and understanding?

Is tradition of equal value to staff, pupils and parents?

Michaela School is a relatively new school in a deprived area of north London, while Sydney Grammar is a long-established independent school in an affluent part of Australia's largest city. Different though they may be in many ways, their staff could be more at home in each other's schools than they would in (outwardly) similar schools. Perhaps then schools can learn much from thinking about the influences they are most shaped by, which may not be limited to location or geography. Their pasts might be fundamental to their present identity, but so too might be the value systems that their staff, and the societies in which they function, hold at any one time. Schools like Harrow School Hong Kong, which have their origins in a very different country from the country they function in, exist conterminously with their society. Do they promote the traditions and values of their 'parent' school or those of their host communities? What happens if they are at odds with each other?

Schools have perhaps always contained a vast range of differing world views. The interviewees suggest that people with different perspectives can still work together through a shared sense of purpose (the need to educate young people). Interviewees differed in what that purpose might look like. For example, how much is a teacher's role about conveying subject knowledge, or bringing about change in society?

For Katharine Birbalsingh, the spread of child-centred learning has resulted in a major change in the dynamic between teacher and pupil, and the long-term consequences to society have been significant. By removing the teacher from the front of the classroom, by re-configuring the seating plan so that the classroom is filled with desks and chairs that are facing inward in groups, the school may, consciously or otherwise, have abdicated adult control. For others, pursuing enquiry-based learning and having the teacher as one of many sources of information is liberating.

The philosopher Susan Neiman (2023) asks:

'Which do you find more essential: the accidents we are born with, or the principles we consider and uphold? Traditionally, it was the Right who focused on the first, and the Left who emphasised the second. This tradition has been inverted.'

Whether or not you agree with such a statement, the questions it raises are worth exploring if you work in a school. What pasts do we promote? Who decides on what should be valued? The parents? The staff? The pupils? Agreeing on the answers requires sensitivity and empathy.

In a world of flux, the interviewees in this chapter have argued that there is a need for the traditional as much as a need for innovation: both may help us find solutions to the challenges we have; furthermore, they may also provide us with the stepping stones we need to get across this most tumultuous of rivers.

Chapter 4

Schools with a focus on creativity

For much of his life, Sir Ken Robinson was best known among educational policy makers as the Chair of the 1997 commission for the new Labour government on creativity in schools. The report he delivered, 'All Our Futures: Creativity, culture and education' (Robinson, 1999), was well-received, but its recommendations were not widely implemented. And then in 2006, Robinson's 19-minute TED talk, 'Do schools kill creativity?' appeared to change the debate around schools and creativity in many countries and turned him into a global phenomenon. Robinson argued that the conventional school model was broken. He put forward the idea that classrooms should be places of innovation, collaboration and imagination, not repositories for rows of desks, where siloed subjects are taught to prepare children for end-of-year, high-stakes examinations. The voice of 'All Our Futures' had found a new platform and a much more receptive audience than Whitehall, online. YouTube, it seemed, was the perfect stage for promoting the idea that inspiration was disruptive and liberating and that rules were confining and stultifying.

Of course, the debate about creativity and rules pre-dates Robinson's talk. Indeed, one can find examples of this dichotomy in any era, and in most disciplines. For example, Plato's 'Ion' is an exploration of the relationship between inspiration and the essential existence of rules that govern the domain of knowledge. Socrates' analysis in this work invites the reader to contemplate the extent to which expertise in any subject is dependent on knowing its rules.

Robinson was opposed to what he saw as the industrialisation and commodification of education. In Robinson and Aronica's 2015 book, *Creative Schools*, he compares modern schools to 'abattoirs', slaughterhouses of the imagination which suppress creativity, imagination and individuality. Robinson's 'revolution' was 'based on a belief in the value of the individual, the right to self-determination, our potential to evolve and live a fulfilled life, and the importance of civic responsibility and respect for others' (Robinson & Aronica, 2015, p. xxii).

Robinson's critics point out that it is one thing to criticise standardised testing or compare schools to factories, and quite another thing to come up with a workable alternative that does not advantage the already privileged children coming from homes filled with cultural capital (see Birbalsingh, 2021). And many challenge the idea of an educational system deliberately using principles from mass production. American commentators Jack Schneider and Jennifer Berkshire, for example, claim that 'the "factory model" metaphor [is] trotted out so often that it [becomes] casually accepted as historical fact' but 'at no point did policy makers collectively determine a model of any sort, much less one based on American industry.' (Cited in Strauss, 2020). In the United Kingdom, Michael Gove, speaking in 2012 when he was Secretary of State for Education, also attacked the idea of factory schools:

'Critics sometimes talk about certain schools as exam factories – dull Gradgrindian institutions which churn out great GCSE and A level passes but which are otherwise joyless prison houses of the soul where the cultivation of the whole child is neglected if not actively scorned.

But I have to say I have never encountered such a school – either in visits or Ofsted reports. Because they don't exist.'

(The phrase 'Gradgrindian' refers to a character from Charles Dickens' novel *Hard Times* in which the character Thomas Gradgrindian is single-minded in his analysis of data, to the detriment of anything creative.)

For Robinson (2019), creativity is 'the process of developing ideas that are original and of value'. How can we decide what is new *and* valuable, and what is simply, at best, novelty and at worst, valueless? David Didau (2014) wrote in response to Robinson: 'We can imagine loads of stuff without actually creating anything worthwhile. It's not creative to come up with ridiculous, impractical nonsense; it's creative to work within boundaries.' Thomas Edison's claim that 'genius is one percent inspiration and ninety-nine percent perspiration' (cited in Rosanoff, 1932) is often quoted too. Writers such as Malcolm Gladwell, in *Outliers* (2008) and Anders Ericcson and Robert Pool in *Peak* (2016) assert that practice and expertise are fundamental to creative success. David Gajadharsingh, principal of the Royal Ballet School (interviewed later in this chapter) suggests: 'You can be creative without a secure understanding of certain foundational rules but the outcomes might not match the initial ideas and/or vision. The development of the work will, almost certainly, be laborious and chaotic, if foundational rules of the process are not understood.' Vibe Esdahl-Schou from Østerskov Efterskole seems to think along similar lines: 'I do believe you can be creative without being an expert in the field, but at the same time creativity calls for bending the rules, challenging them… which raises the question: Do you have to know the rules to bend them?' Others might focus on a child's natural capacity for goodness, creativity and empathetic learning, and see this at the heart of an authentic education. This is a view perhaps first espoused in Rousseau's *Emile* (1762) and continued, to varying degrees, in the work of highly influential educationalists such as Jean Piaget and Lev Vygotsky.

In 2019, a year before he died, Robinson wrote that politicians had been suffocating schools in a repressing 'culture of standardisation'. Because of this, he claimed, the qualities that young people need if they are to contribute to a more equitable world ('creativity, compassion, citizenship and collaboration') have been neglected. In the view of *The Guardian* (2019), the 2019 Durham Commission on Creativity and Education in England was set up in response to this sort of concern. This Commission attempted to find a common set of definitions for creativity in a school setting. The Committee, chaired by former Director of Tate Modern, Sir Nicholas Serota, agreed on these definitions:

Creativity: The capacity to imagine, conceive, express, or make something that was not there before.
Creative thinking: A process through which knowledge, intuition and skills are applied to imagine, express or make something novel or individual in its contexts. Creative thinking is present in all areas of life. It may appear spontaneous, but it can be underpinned by perseverance, experimentation, critical thinking and collaboration.
Teaching for creativity: Explicitly using pedagogies and practices that cultivate creativity in young people.

The Durham Commission has a legacy in the 'Creativity Exchange' project (www.cre ativityexchange.org.uk) although its recommendations have not led to significant changes in England's education policy. Later on in this chapter we will explore various schools' definitions and conceptions of creativity and what that looks like in their settings.

What about the question of assessment in schools in relation to creativity? Many might consider children in England to be over-examined and that this might therefore be an argument against standardised testing. However, Daisy Christodoulou (2014, p.99) has said: 'just because our children are overexamined, it does not necessarily follow that they must therefore be overburdened with knowledge...It is a mistake to view English school-leaving examinations as being Gradgrindian tests of lists of facts'. Ken Robinson was not against all standardised assessments ('if I go for a medical examination, I want some standardized tests, not some idiosyncratic scale my doctor made up', quoted in Strauss, 2015). When the UK government's Task Group on Assessment and Testing published its proposals for a framework for the reporting of national curriculum results in 1987 it set out why attainment targets are necessary. For the authors of the proposals, they 'establish what children should normally be expected to know, understand and be able to do at around the ages of 7, 11, 14 and 16 and will enable the progress of each child to be measured against established national standards. They will reflect what pupils must achieve to progress in their education and to become thinking and informed people.' (Cited in Wiliam, 2001, p. 2).

Perhaps the question then is not whether we should be testing creativity but rather what method of testing it objectively differentiates between what is valuable and what is not. For Michael Gove (2012), memorisation liberates rather than destroys creativity in young people:

'Memorisation is a necessary pre-condition of understanding – only when facts and concepts are committed securely to the memory – so that it is no effort to recall them and no effort is required to work things out from first principles – do we really have a secure hold on knowledge. Memorising scales, or times tables, or verse, so that we can play, recall or recite automatically gives us this mental equipment to perform more advanced functions and display greater creativity.'

Psychologists Jeffrey Smith and Lisa Smith once wrote:

'Creativity and education sit and look at one another from a distance, much like the boys and girls at the seventh-grade dance, each one knowing that a foray across the gym floor might bring great rewards but is fraught with peril.' (Quoted in Lucas et al., 2012, p. 5)

The schools we have talked to have attempted to not just narrow that distance but to cross it. Rather than instilling a mistrust of innovation, they have sought to encourage an embracing of difference and ideas. They put creativity at the core of their identities and come from a range of contexts and with a wide interpretation of what creativity is. We wanted to know their views on the importance of creativity, how that creativity is promoted in their school, if the children they teach benefit from the emphasis they place on creativity, and whether other areas suffer as a result. We ask the schools interviewed whether they feel they can successfully make creativity central to their identities, if every child's innate talent can be drawn out and if all pupils can be genuinely creative.

Royal Ballet School

Fact file

Number of pupils: 222

Age range: 11–19

Co-educational/Single sex: Co-educational

Location: UK

State-funded/Independent: Independent

When was it established? 1926

Head/Contributor: David Gajadharsingh (Academic and Pastoral Principal)

Our pupils come from: A wide range of backgrounds from the UK and around the world. Pupils are offered a place solely on their talent and potential in classical ballet. Over 80% of students receive financial support from either the Department for Education or other external donors. The school is part of the Music and Dance Scheme (www.gov.uk/music-dance-scheme).

Our values: Striving for excellence, nurturing individuals, actively widening access, our heritage nourishes our future, and always innovating.

In the future: We hope to influence the wider world of ballet by promoting the very best aspects of our training and healthcare programme as well as our innovative professional development programme for new and experienced ballet teachers.

The importance of creativity

Creativity is about allowing students to explore their own ideas and working with others to produce work which is original, innovative, challenging and entertaining.

The school has introduced a range of choreography modules into the curriculum and brought in specialist choreographic teachers to assist the students in their creative process. The school has invested in a continuing professional development programme for all artistic staff which is closely linked to what is available for academic teachers in their induction period. This has empowered the artistic teachers to move to a more collaborative and student-centred approach to their artistic teaching. The focus is now one of 'teaching' rather than 'instructing'.

How is creativity promoted?

Creativity can be taught. Students can learn how the creative process might work for them and they can model their behaviours on experts in the field. This builds confidence, resilience and allows the students to take risks with their work; pushing the boundaries for them and their dancers and hence taking the journey of exploration to new areas.

I believe that all children can be creative. The key is to show them what others have produced and achieved with their work. Children are exceptional learners and if one can show them what has been done, how their peers have done it, and then allow the children to explore ideas for themselves in a safe and secure space where mistakes are seen as normal and outcomes are welcomed in a positive manner, they all have the opportunity to learn to create.

Empowering teachers to be creative might be a more difficult goal to achieve, given the resistance to change that some teachers exhibit. Teachers need to see the benefits of the changes before they adopt new practices. This will involve visits to other schools/classes and interrogation of the techniques used. The use of vocational schools in this aspect might be very helpful. The positive benefits to student engagement, learning and progress through exposure to a range of creative and performing arts is a feature of such schools.

You can be creative without a secure understanding of certain foundational rules, but the outcomes might not match the initial ideas and/or vision. The development of the work will, almost certainly, be laborious and chaotic if foundational rules of the process are not understood.

Creativity is about the freedom to explore and produce innovative outcomes. Some examples might be:

(a) the production of a piece of theatre in another language

(b) devising an experiment to show a particular property of an element in chemistry, or coming up with a new way to capture some data in the lab

(c) devising a mathematical game or writing computer code to accomplish a task.

One can assess the outcomes and gauge the quality of the progress made from start to finish; taking into account use of resources, management/motivation of others, time management and quality of outcome.

As for assessing creativity formally: I would not be keen, as the students may then see it as just another test. The joy of seeing the final piece come to life is normally a far better motivator than a grade. Praise, sharing with others and celebration across a wide audience are more desirable.

A more courageous approach to teaching needs to be developed nationally; one in which the aspects outlined above can be developed without the pressures of external exams getting in the way. A different approach to the format and style of some examination questions could support this.

What is lost by emphasising creativity so much?

As a vocational school, we develop creativity in much of our curriculum through dance. We also offer traditional Key Stage 3 and GCSE courses in art, music and drama. The students bring these skills to their learning and despite our truly comprehensive intake, they secure impressive results (see the Independent Schools

Inspectorate report for the school, 2022). And, genuinely, as the school is set up to be creative we have not had any challenges, as we have not had to make sacrifices. The academic teachers moan about missing lessons of course but, ultimately, given the results are so good, the system seems to work.

However, compared to a non-vocational school, we have a reduced GCSE diet (eight subjects is the typical load, rather than ten, and a reduced curriculum in terms of subjects studied and options available at GCSE). We also don't offer traditional A levels in the sixth form: students do a degree programme (validated by the University of Roehampton) which is 70% performance based. However, we are a vocational school, so we would never have had the option to offer the same range of subjects as other schools. Hence, there is no sacrifice.

Østerskov Efterskole

Fact file

Number of pupils: 92

Age range: 14–18

Co-educational/Single sex: Co-educational

Location: Denmark

State-funded/Independent: Partly state-funded, partly independently funded

When was it established? 2006

Head/Contributor: Vibe Esdahl-Schou (Head of Strategy, Learning and Innovation)

Our pupils come from: All over Denmark. Our students are often gifted (IQs well above average) and they often lack motivation to learn through the public school system. They just don't see the point in learning just to pass an exam. In addition, up to 30% of our students are on the autism spectrum. Up to 25% of our students have suffered from extended school non-attendance. Most of those students have also experienced severe stress or signs of depression as a result of that. Up to 25% of our students come from low-income homes. Up to 75% of our students have experienced severe bullying in their former schools.

Our values: Agency, adventure seeking, tolerance and immersion. Østerskov Efterskole is a Danish efterskole, i.e. a boarding school for grades 9–10. An efterskole is a 200-year-old Danish concept. An efterskole is set free from the rules and regulations that the public school system has to adhere to, which means that we, among other things, have freedom of method. We can teach however we please, as long as we properly prepare the students for the same exams as the public school system.

Our academic vision: Our vision and philosophy is to teach complex subjects through play, games and role-playing. Our school motto is *Scientia per ludum* (learning through play). We want to make learning fun again. All subjects are taught through week-long role plays or games, each set in a new narrative framework or universe. The students inhabit that universe for the week and experiment, compete and cooperate to succeed in the game/role play. All lessons are taught as part of the overall narrative. The knowledge gained from the lessons can be directly linked and used in the game.

In the future: We hope to make our method more accessible to teachers in the public school system. We are constantly developing new ideas and concepts, and our next big project is to offer courses to supplement the teachers' education.

The importance of creativity

Creativity means the freedom to explore and act. Our students explore the world and their own identity through games, play and role play, and we teach them to be curious, act, adapt and search for common ground and compromises. I would argue that committing something to memory by repetition can be done in a creative way, rather than just repetitive patterns. For instance, when our students work with equations in maths, they are playing the roles of witch hunters in 17th-century Salem. At first they are taught the basics: the teacher explains it, demonstrates on the blackboard, etc. But, rather than ask the students to practise by doing 100 equations as an assignment to hand in, we ask them to use their new knowledge immediately. Solving equations becomes part of an elaborate board game, where the witch hunters can move around the board by experimenting with equations. They each choose a basic equation to work from and then they will experiment with substituting varying elements of the equation to be able to make the moves they need to catch the witch.

Our own approach has developed, but not changed. However, the world around us has changed in the sense that they are more open to our approach and no longer question *if* you can learn through our approach.

How is creativity promoted?

I don't believe you can teach creativity. You can enable it. The most important thing is to provide an environment in which it is safe to take risks and to explore without the fear of failure. Because all children can be creative: creativity is not an ability, but a mindset. And you develop a mindset by providing the right environment in which to cultivate it.

In the early years of the school, some children left because they did not feel it was right for them. Efterskolers are semi-private schools, meaning that we decide for ourselves which students we want to admit to the school. Before enrolling with us, we conduct an interview with each prospective student to make sure that they know what they are signing up for. In recent years, we have become better at marketing our school based on our method of teaching. Nowadays, the students who apply to us do so because we are different and because they want something other than the public school system.

Luckily, our teachers are much the same as our students: they apply to work for us because of how we do things and because they want to work in a creative teaching environment. In my opinion (derived from numerous conversations with teachers working in the public school system), creativity and courage will thrive if you provide the right nutrients. If, as a teacher, you are overworked and constantly being measured on your (or rather, your students') results, by your supervisors or by the system in general, then you are going to play it safe and teach as you yourself were taught. If, however, you are encouraged to experiment, if we remove the fear of failure and redefine the measures of success, then you will be freer to explore. I think creativity benefits from a certain understanding and genuine appreciation of your medium (for example, a profound love of language in a writer). I do believe you can be creative without being an expert in the field, but at the same time creativity calls for bending the rules, challenging them… which raises the question: Do you have to know the rules to bend them?

I fundamentally disagree with the premise that creativity can be measured. All children can be creative, but not all children will become the next Picasso. 'Genius' may require prior knowledge, and yes, geniuses are often creative *beyond* measure. But I do not believe that 'secure knowledge' is a prerequisite for being creative. I tend to lean in the opposite direction: too many rules will most likely inhibit creativity. You don't measure creativity; you feel it.

We do not measure progress in our students' creativity, nor do we grade them for their creativity. Because we have to follow the standards of the public school system, we grade the students based on their knowledge and performance in the exams. We teach them in a creative way, making it more fun to learn.

Let me give you an example using our *Peace in our Time* project.

The students are divided into nine different fictional nations. The diplomacy, intrigue and controversies bear an uncanny resemblance to real-life events. The students play the roles as head of state and the officials as well as the general population. Each nation is awarded different points and advantages depending on their infrastructure, their form of government, their stance on human rights and environmental issues, etc. For instance, if you choose to be a dictatorship, it will be easier for you to make decisions during the UN summits but, at the same time, your population is more likely to rebel, causing your infrastructure to collapse. During the week, the students are taught how to govern a small country. In their history and social studies lessons, they will read about the political climate during the Cold War and tie that to current events, prompting them to reflect on their decision-making process and the political effects of those decisions. In maths, they will learn about budgets, GNP [Gross National Product] and how to use and read statistics, enabling them to attend meetings at the World Bank. In chemistry, they will learn about fertiliser, enabling them to boost their food production to keep the population happy. Every lesson has a purpose and the students will see an immediate effect to gaining that new knowledge. During the week, the students will debate matters of international importance, they will make allies and enemies, all the while keeping their nation's best interest in mind. Aside from teaching the subjects, the teachers act as game masters and they will push certain agendas to bring our simulation even closer to real-world events.

When they begin with us, our students range from below average to well above average. The students with a low grade point average will improve during their year with us, landing within the median of the national grade point average. The students with high marks will usually be able to maintain them, while at the same time stating that they have felt challenged and motivated to learn for the first time in years.

What is lost by emphasising creativity so much?

No sacrifice is needed. Creativity is an inherent part of our school DNA. I think our students leave our school knowing as much about conventional subjects as students who attend more 'mainstream' schools. Apart from doing quite well at the exams, most of our students go on to higher education and when they return to visit us, they unanimously say that the most important thing they learned at Østerskov is that knowledge and learning is fun, and that we taught them to be independent thinkers. When I speak to high school teachers who have taught some of our former students, they say that Østerskov students are more responsible, more curious and more focused on cooperation than the average high school student. In my opinion, that is more important than being able to recite the curriculum. You can always catch up on knowledge, if you have the agency to do so, and that's what we teach them.

The biggest challenge we face is fighting for some kind of legitimacy within the school system. We have had to constantly explain and justify our chosen method of teaching because people did not believe you could learn *and* have fun at the same time. Now, 17 years in, we can document that our students meet the national grade point average, that our students' grades improve during their year with us and that they do just as well as everyone else when they go on to high school, etc. And that is quite an achievement, considering a lot of our students were fed up with school and suffered from extended school non-attendance before they enrolled with us.

Nanjing International School

Fact file

Number of pupils: 625

Age range: 4–18

Co-educational/Single sex: Co-educational

Location: China

State-funded/Independent: Independent

When was it established? 1992

Head/Contributor: Laurie (Laurence) McLellan (Director)

Our pupils come from: All over the world. We currently have about 30 nationalities on campus. We are referred to by the Chinese authorities as a 'school for the children of foreign experts'. A strategic focus for us is 'inclusion, with an emphasis on diversity'. We therefore have a cap on the number of students holding any one passport at 30%. Our largest groups are Korean (always at 30% with a waiting list), Chinese heritage (heterogeneous group with multiple passports, but mainly from the USA) about 35% and German 6% There is a smaller selection of other nationalities.

Our values: Inclusion, international-mindedness, personal excellence and creative thinking. Our strategy is: 'Student voice and student choice' and 'Burst the bubble!'

Our academic and pastoral vision: We take personal excellence very seriously. We see academics as being an element of personal development, but refute the Grade 12 exam outcomes as the only measure of student, and hence school, success. We expect everyone to reach their personal best and celebrate that at graduation; however, we see this as the minimum standard, and to be frank, a less interesting aspect of success. We are deeply committed to making the journey important for students and working on skills, attributes and dispositions that prepare them for success in life. We see creativity – not just super ideas, but super problem recognition and problem-solving – as being the essence of this endeavour.

In the future: We hope to improve. We are involved in a long-term internal redesign of learning spaces to match our mission and strategy. We are cognisant of the space being the 'Third Teacher', while accepting that great learning depends most on the quality of teachers and the culture/ethos of the school.

The importance of creativity

To me, creativity is at the core of individual or group expression, innovation, passion and discovery.

Nanjing International School (NIS) states, in our mission, that we aim to inspire creative thinking. In 2011, we created a new mission statement following a broad consultation process with community members present and past. We delved deep into the Why? of our school. We realised that the school was innovative and prepared to try new things, in a manner of speaking, to take risks. However, we felt a weakness was a lack of creativity in the learning process and learning outputs, because most of our community thought that creativity resided exclusively within music, visual and performing arts. What creative thinking means to NIS is that there is a way of unlocking the potential in all students and teachers, all learners.

NIS worked with a consultancy called NoTosh to help us, as we saw creative thinking as our weakness. They helped us find architects to redesign our school to match our educational beliefs, and to develop a strategy to help bring our mission to life. In 2016, we launched our school strategy: 'Student voice and choice' and 'Burst the bubble'. In 2020, we launched our second iteration of the strategy with more simple definitions and a call to action. Our view is that all children should be able to understand our strategy rather than just adults. We want all learners, students and teachers to live the strategy rather than adults doing it to and for children. (Important side note: we do not have a strategic plan; we ditched that whole concept 10 years ago. We engage in strategic thinking which is directional rather than a list of 'to dos'.)

How is creativity promoted?

Is it possible to teach creativity? Yes, as long as you do not think it is a subject! Creativity is more an approach, a way of thinking and being, than a set of content. In the same way that we are all language teachers regardless of our subject speciality, to teach creativity all teachers need to have an approach towards teaching and learning that is part of a creative process. And all children are creative: it is part of our nature as humans. We have to stop thinking that only some children are creative and others are not. The same goes for teachers, although admittedly there can be new learning and, indeed, unlearning for some to be able to recognise the creativity they have as individuals. It needs a whole-school approach for existing teachers and a focus for future recruitment.

It is important to stop thinking of school as a set of subjects or disciplines. If teachers define themselves by their discipline first, and as educators second, the journey for a school to optimise the latent creativity within the faculty can be challenging. When we went to implement our new strategy, the group, some of whom were department heads, realised that a siloed hierarchy of department heads was going to be an impediment to a strategy that needed a flatter structure of leadership. You can become a brilliant writer without knowing all the rules of grammar. However, your writing would improve significantly with knowledge of grammar and writing structures. In the creative process, the freedom to experiment is enhanced by skill development.

We have to stop defining creativity in narrow, subject-based language. Chemistry, maths and economics are full of creativity in their past, present and hopefully the future. Look for the process, the innovation, the change over time or the sudden change – creativity will be part of it. The ability of humans to think out of the box, to experiment, to wonder, to discover and to invent... This discussion is not about subjects or disciplines at the core; however they can help us understand different contexts for creativity and then to see the patterns of similarity of approach.

We have a tendency as educators to be innovative in our ideas about learning and stuck in old, rather basic, ways of measuring outputs. This is the hard end of the conversation about creativity; well-designed surveys of perceptions/attitudes/experiences for students, listening focus groups for students using a protocol that gives everyone in the group equal voice, or at least access (equity) to express themselves. This approach needs to be consistent over time, to produce data that should, in turn, lead to new questions about creativity at the school. We shouldn't formally assess creativity.

As a believer in inclusion and inclusive practices, my view is that all teachers should be teaching and creating learning experiences that benefit/engage all learners. By seeing students as being from a certain 'background' or 'ability range', you're already heading down the wrong path. With the exception of language acquisition (90% of our students do not speak English with their families at home) and maths classes, in Grades 9–12 we have no tiered/setted system, or whatever other system exists, which labels students as being at a certain level.

What is lost by emphasising creativity so much?

We used the design thinking methodology from Stanford d.school (design school) at the start of our journey. I took a Stanford course and was intrigued that at the Stanford d.school they do not teach design as a discrete subject. Their whole push is to use a methodology that brings specialists in different academic disciplines together to solve problems. I wondered how we could do that at NIS. Our first mission-driven construction project was to create a design centre. We made design a compulsory class for all Grade 6–10 students. We then constructed a Design Pit in primary and all students in Grades 1–10 have compulsory design classes every week. Design gets the same amount of lesson time as other subjects. I guess it has become one of our USPs. Design is not a place for tinkering; it is a place to use the design cycle, to help solve real problems, sometimes for real clients.

I guess we sacrificed lessons from four other subjects to create the time on the schedule. There was so much excitement and buy-in to us recognising the need for these skills, such as the reports from the World Economic Forum, the Board acceptance that they have lots of young graduates from the 'best' universities in their companies (BASF, Bosch-Siemens, Ford, LG, Samsung) who live in their heads and have so few practical skills. They saw design, the nurturing of creativity to solve problems, as 'real-life' school.

You need to use research, show real-life examples, learn yourself and to have a simple, but deep, message. You also need to be able to maintain confidence in what you already offer without being compromised. We have strong academic outcomes, good university placement and great confidence in the school being 'edgy'. I was offering something extra in the experience, not a replacement. Our academics are still strong; however we now have more students deciding to study in areas that are commonly referred to in the British context as 'creative industries'. Some of these students are our highest performing academic students, who see areas such as engineering in a broader context. We have film makers, game designers, fashion designers with a commitment to sustainability. It's incremental with our doctors, lawyers, scientists, mathematicians still following their path, but hopefully with a different mindset. Without being arrogant, our alumni in the UK, USA, Australia, Germany, Netherlands and Canada comment on how their classmates are fine with academics and lost with how to work in teams, take on challenges, present a pitch, challenge the status quo and enjoy learning. Proud, moi? You'd better believe it!

The BRIT School

Fact file

Number of pupils: 1,400

Age range: 14–19

Co-educational/Single sex: Co-educational

Location: UK

State-funded/Independent: State- and grant-funded

When was it established? 1991

Head/Contributor: Stuart Worden (Principal)

Our pupils come from: Our local community and greater London. 10% come from beyond this catchment area. There are no academic criteria for entry. 45% of our students are from the global majority and there are an above average number of students who have additional educational needs.

Our values: Be original, responsible, ambitious, inclusive and kind, and our decisions are based on these.

Our vision and philosophy: To skill young people to take careers in the creative and performing arts industries. The BRIT school is a specialist vocational arts training school. It is free and inclusive.

In the future: We hope to still be here and for other schools to have deep and enriching arts curriculums.

The importance of creativity

All humans are creative, and along with empathy, creativity is the super power that the world needs right now. Consequently it is central to all our decisions, our structures, our pedagogy and our heartbeat.

I think the pandemic gave creativity a new energy and encouraged a combination of creative communities and creativity autonomy. The significant change in the last five years has been the decreasing investment in creative education by both the government and the education system. This is a shame.

Rather than teaching creativity, you can give it a place in education and you can encourage creativity. Our experience at the school is that some students have a narrow view of their creativity. For example, a dancer may think they are only skilled at ballet. Our training offers multiple opportunities for creativity. For instance, ballet dancers will be encouraged to do street, jazz and tap, and you would hope that their creativity would therefore expand. The other important part of teaching creativity is to have faith in a polymathic approach. So, the ballet dancer who expands into other forms of dance is also encouraged to study dance for camera and thus they develop their creative skills and knowledge of another art form.

How is creativity promoted?

The notion of play and risk are central to the development of successful humans and communities. If schools can encourage risk, failure and the ensemble through play and adventure, all children could be creative. It needs to be valued and nurtured through the ethos inside a school setting. Teachers really shouldn't be in the profession if they are not creative or open to the adventures of creativity. Creativity does not exclude any neurological status but rather improves all and everyone.

Educational practice should be encouraged to develop caution about the rules of an art form. For instance, many writers now question the use of capital letters as patriarchal. Kae Tempest is one such writer, as is debbie tucker green; debbie tucker green will only write in lower case. Some of the more revolutionary creatives and approaches (punk, Picasso, Kendrick) have frequently questioned rules and regulations. Contrary to this view, The BRIT School also has huge faith in the constructs of an art form, i.e. the importance of reading music in order to create new art forms.

How we measure, or evaluate, creativity is not so easy to answer. Some of the metrics may be around the value of happiness that the creative feels. For example, has the actor's creativity increased the happiness of the creator? I don't think the sales of a record, or where something appears in a bestseller list, tell us everything about their value. Measuring creativity is difficult, but what we can say is that the creativity industries are the biggest provider to the UK economy and the fastest growing sector in all industries at present, so we can be confident that creativity as a 'product' is being consumed more than ever before. But creativity is a state of mind; actions and behaviours rather than a metric.

What is lost by emphasising creativity so much?

Nothing. There are presumptions on us and many schools, I suspect, to reduce creativity in the curriculum, but I think that this is a regressive view of what creativity is. For instance, our maths department is frequently taking a creative approach towards their subject and I recently witnessed a science experiment on how the mixing of alkaline and acid created a rainbow and consequently celebrated the EDI (equality, diversity and inclusion) ethos of the school. So, I don't think that the binary view that there is academia on one hand and creativity on the other is helpful. I don't think any school has to sacrifice anything; rather it highlights creativity and acknowledges its liberating capability. Sadly, from my understanding of certain curriculum leads in core subjects, creativity is on the downward trend in many schools.

Success in our students in employment (98%, including 70+% in the creative industries) would indicate that we are doing the right thing; we are championing creativity in the curriculum and in our values. However, the current funding of vocational creative education is not at the level it needs to be, to deliver the standards required by industry. Consequently, there are some challenges ahead. An inclusive talent pipeline, that has people from all backgrounds versed in creativity, will get narrower, and the implications of that are concerning.

Another view

Here, Ian Warwick explores the idea that creativity is not merely the remit of 'artistic' subjects. Perhaps counter-intuitively and (to foreshadow his science analogy) there is a debatable benefit in providing rigid foundations (solids) against which creativity can bounce (gases) and through which it can flow (liquids) in order to enhance the potential of the creative and academic approaches so that each complements the other. He posits that the two should not be mutually exclusive but should work together to create – in effect – new synapses in education.

Ian Warwick, ex-teacher and founder of London Gifted & Talented

What fuels our original thinking?

In the 15th century, Pacioli asserted that without mathematics there is no art. Many centuries later, Max Planck, the father of quantum theory, expanded this idea when he wrote that the pioneer scientist must have a vivid intuitive imagination for new ideas, 'not generated simply by deduction, but by an artistically creative imagination' (Planck, 1950, p. 109).

We know that the mind functions on several hierarchic levels at once, and often one level does not know what the other is doing. What both thinkers might be suggesting is that the essence of the creative act is bringing them together. Essentially, the 'freewheeling' creative subjects do not hold a monopoly over the so-called 'precise' sciences, particularly with regard to our willingness to surrender preconceptions, to abandon our frozen thinking. All subjects have a deep seated drive to interrogate, to integrate, to find patterns, create or expose hidden analogies and ultimately to uncover solutions. But creativity needs a bump start, an idea or a way of seeing, which sets off our own generative processes.

So where do we find an ideas space, a more creative perspective?

A simple metaphor might help to illustrate what has become this increasingly tedious 'liberal versus traditional' dilemma on creativity. We know that as a gas, matter is chaotic and volatile. There is too much anarchy. As a solid, matter is stable but inflexible. It is unlikely to change or adapt, as there is too much order. In between, there is the potential for more liquid networks where new connections and new ideas have an opportunity to take shape. This is a place where, according to computer scientist, Christopher Langton (1990), understanding is not fixed, but neither is it unstable: where ideas can connect and, as a result, new possibilities and patterns might be more available to be explored.

However, in the 21st century, the paths we are encouraged to take tend to lead us towards becoming specialists (and therefore probably reductionists). So, perhaps we need a different driver to explore the intersections between the artistic subjects, maths and an entire range of sciences.

Thinking aside

[French philosopher Étienne] Souriau (1892–1979) asserted that to invent, you must 'think aside'. He may well have been illustrating the potential of the 'adjacent possible' (Kaufman, 1995, 2000). This forms a kind of shadow future, hovering on the edges of the present state of things, a map of all the ways in which the present can reinvent itself. We need to do more than encourage new ideas, we need to help set up 'collisions' between ideas: the collisions that happen when different fields of expertise converge in some shared physical or intellectual space.

When the situation you face is blocked, straight thinking must be superseded by a new auxiliary matrix which will unblock it. Originality emerges from a productive collision of ideas, across traditional subjects. But in order to invent, you have to be willing to live with a sense of uncertainty, to work in darkness and grope towards an answer, even to put up with the anxiety about whether there is an answer [at all]. In 'The Crack Up' F. Scott Fitzgerald noted that a test of a keen intelligence is the ability to hold two opposing ideas in your mind at the same time and to know that both are true (referenced in Blumberg, 2011). The British mathematician, AN Whitehead, was purported to have claimed that we can fly 'in poetry and music' whilst at the same time using our knowledge of 'quantity and number' as anchors for those uplifting new ideas and discoveries (quoted by MacTutor, no date). Both believed that creativity does not exist in a vacuum, that it's difficult to rewrite the past without first reading the past. We need to know things, even if those things are ambiguous or even contradictory, before we can attempt to be original.

How do we come up with innovative ideas?

There is no shortcut to understanding. Insights are unfortunately not offered to the ignorant or the talentless or the lazy. Picasso believed in the power of creativity, but drily noted that, 'inspiration exists, but it has to find you working' (cited in Villasante, 1994, p. 264). Being creative should not be a case of benign tolerance of lateral thinking, the unusual or the idiosyncratic. The creative act does not conjure something out of nothing; at best, it uncovers, selects, reshuffles, combines and synthesises already existing facts and ideas. So how can we all think slightly more 'askew'? Thinking aside is a temporary liberation from the tyranny of watertight algorithms, over-precise concepts and the axioms ingrained in the very texture of our language and specialised ways of thought. We can, of course, appreciate creativity simply for its poetic power, beauty or aesthetic pleasure. But more significantly, creativity needs to provide an invaluable way of gaining purchase to elucidate abstract scientific and mathematical concepts. It can, and should, help us to make sense of our world, from metaphysics to mathematics, from science to psychology.

As Lloyd Morgan, the British psychologist believed, it is important to 'saturate yourself through and through with your subject…and wait' (cited in McKeller, 1957, p. 119). We know that progress tends to be neither gradual, linear nor continuous. The breaking down of frontiers between previously unrelated subjects is key. In the same way that there can be a blocked matrix in an individual's mind, the same can be said for various impasses in science and technology. Old orthodoxies need to be confronted.

With greater creative thinking, connections are made. A rival reality is floated into our minds. 'This' might be like 'that', so we can begin to think anew. We picture a likeness, which speeds us towards a new meaning or way of understanding, which can then translate the abstract into a more concrete and graspable understanding. This is the future of education, across all subject areas.

Reflections

How should creativity be represented in schools?

Each of the contributors discussed their school's own unique and fascinating ways of developing creativity. For example, the Royal Ballet School favours a student-centred approach to assist students in their own creative processes, for example in choreography work, experimentation in science or writing computer code. They see the development of creativity being about behaviours as much as anything else: encouraging students to take risks, see mistakes as normal and welcome outcomes for their own and others' work. Experts are brought in who can model these sorts of behaviours. At Østerskov Efterskole there is a particular focus on using the mediums of play and drama, creating challenges and scenarios out of particular tasks to inspire students' imaginations.

What about assessment? Bill Lucas, Guy Claxton and Ellen Spencer (2012, p. 2) argue that until we know how to assess creativity, schools will not put time and resources into teaching it:

'We…need to develop an approach to assessing it [creativity] which is both rigorous enough to ensure credibility *and* user-friendly enough to be used by busy teachers.'

These authors recognise many advantages to assessing creativity, but also see many disadvantages. The advantages they cite include: 'creative-mindedness is seen as an important aspect of the formal curriculum' and 'inspiring teaching' (p. 3). However, they also list disadvantages: 'the idea that young people could come out of school labelled [a] *level 7 imagine*r...is horrific' (p. 10–11). David Gajadharsingh of the Royal Ballet School advocates for considering factors like use of resources, time management, collaboration and quality of outcome for informal assessment but similarly does not support the idea of formal assessment of creativity. Instead he suggests that the focus should be on the 'joy' in seeing a final piece or product, the welcome, praise and celebration with others. At Østerskov Efterskole their students still take the public school system exams and receive grades; the creativity comes in how they learn rather than being part of any formal assessment.

Lucas, Claxton and Spencer accept that 'a central challenge for the cultivation of creativity in schools is their subject-dominated nature' (2012, p. 5). Laurie McLellan, from Nanjing International School, would perhaps agree with that. He said: 'Most of our community thought that creativity resided exclusively within music, visual and performing arts'. Interestingly, their new creative strategy did not work within particular subjects but rather looked beyond and around these to have students involved in their educational beliefs and mission as a school: 'We have to stop defining creativity in narrow, subject-based language'. There are interdisciplinary models, such as the International Baccalaureate Middle Years Programme (MYP), but these have not seen wide uptake with only approximately 1,500 schools offering the MYP (IB World Schools Yearbook, no date).

It is perhaps not the same in primary schools where the emphasis on (and need for) creativity is much more pronounced. Indeed, writers such as Anna Craft have successfully advocated for creativity to be explicitly taught to younger children. Craft's *Creativity Across the Primary Curriculum*, published in 2000, was a seminal text that sought to define the creative act and provide a framework for developing it.

Creativity for its own sake?

Conrad Hughes (Director General of the International School of Geneva and interviewed in Chapter 5) points out that figures such as Thomas Edison, Albert Einstein, Winston Churchill, Richard Branson, Rihanna, Steve Jobs, Lewis Hamilton and Cameron Diaz all had difficulty with a 'rigid' school system but experienced success and found their creative selves. He asserts that creativity is not just innately valuable, but that it makes people more employable. If you work in schools for any length of time you are likely, every few years, to find yourself sitting in an assembly hall listening to a presenter tell you that what employers need in the 21st century are new attributes from those applying to work for them. These might include interpersonal skills, leadership skills, the ability to communicate and collaborate, the ability to 'think outside the box', to be imaginative and, of course, to be creative.

Should creativity in the classroom be an end in itself or is the aim employability? And what might this look like in terms of both teaching and assessment?

Brad Weinstein, founder of TeacherGoals, posted this in 2021 on X (formerly Twitter):

> Employers: We need workers that can think creatively and collaborate well with others.
>
> Government: Let's prioritize standardized tests.
>
> Make it make sense.

Katharine Birbalsingh, the well-known headteacher of Michaela School in London (interviewed in Chapter 3) responded by posting:

> I can make it make sense.
>
> Without testing, the kids won't learn anything, which means they won't know anything to be creative with. 👍

Which in turn provoked a response from Dylan Wiliam, arguably one of the most influential educationalists writing today:

> A real problem with a lot of writing on creativity is that it ignores the second part of the standard definition [sic]: having novel ideas that have value. Blowing through the wrong end of a trumpet is not creative; Miles Davis is. Creativity almost always requires disciplinary mastery.

The question that emerged from the ensuing debate, and which we can see in the schools that feature in this chapter, is one of utility. Should creativity be useful? Should it have, as Craft (2000) has argued, an outcome which makes it innately more valuable than if it was not awarded one?

Perhaps one could argue that schools will not or cannot be as creative as Ken Robinson wanted them to be, but that does not mean they are not being creative at a lesson-by-lesson level and in spontaneous moments of interaction, as well as through schemes of work and even in examination halls. And whatever else, the requirement for governments to acknowledge the critical importance of subjects historically seen as the petri dishes for creativity (art, drama, music, dance) as core parts of the school curriculum and not marginal nice-to-haves, feels like an absolutely critical outcome not just for all those who advocate for more creativity in learning, but for all who care about cultural development and beauty in society.

Not every school will be the Østerskov Efterskole, but arguably every single child should have spaces kept safe and prioritised in their learning week, to flex their imaginations and creative muscles, in culturally exciting and experientially stimulating ways.

Schools like The BRIT School, the Royal Ballet School, Nanjing International School and Østerskov Efterskole meet a need and find their own way of supporting the children they teach. They also represent and argue for varied and powerful expressions of creativity in schools. To expect any monolithic state to sanction the teaching of something so subjective and intangible as creativity, to assess it across all disciplines and to find consistent ways of marking and standardising it, would perhaps be counterproductive. State-approved and graded creativity sounds like a recipe for something dull, prescribed, approved and derivative, positioned to hit assessment objectives rather than to express something new and valued. In the school ecosystem perhaps it is conceivably better (to use a cliché, rather than something more creative) to see a thousand flowers bloom, than to cultivate one bright, but bland, field.

Chapter 5

Developing curricula and assessment

The taught curriculum is arguably at the heart of everything the school does: which authors are read, which scientific topics are assessed, which periods of history are studied, which languages are learned. The school leaders interviewed in this chapter have each carefully considered what needs to be covered in their curriculum and have no doubt had to ask difficult questions along the way. Which topics need to be covered in more depth? Which topics should be replaced, and in which subjects? What metrics should be employed to make these sorts of decisions? Who judges which changes are worthwhile and of lasting educational merit? What sort of curricula might both prepare pupils for and also serve the societies they will enter as adults? For what types of occupations and professions should schools perhaps be equipping their pupils?

Some might argue for a focus on particular skills to prepare students for their work and citizenship in the future. Andreas Schleicher (2012), Director of the Directorate of Education and Skills and the OECD, writes:

'Education today is much more about ways of thinking which involve creative and critical approaches to problem-solving and decision-making. It is also about ways of working, including communication and collaboration, as well as the tools they require, such as the capacity to recognise and exploit the potential of new technologies, or indeed, to avert their risks. And last but not least, education is about the capacity to live in a multi-faceted world as an active and engaged citizen. These citizens influence what they want to learn and how they want to learn it, and it is this that shapes the role of educators.'

A focus on skills may not necessarily mean removing knowledge and content from the curriculum however. Dan Willingham asserts that 'the sorts of skills that teachers want from students – such as the ability to analyse and to think critically – *require* extensive factual knowledge' (2010, p. 26). What needs to be taught then, and how? Should the curriculum be assessed and, if so, how can this be done fairly, reliably and rigorously?

There are other difficulties when it comes to creating a perfect curriculum. For example, the human brain – even when it is being paid to do so – finds it difficult to focus for very long on thinking. 'Compared to your ability to see and move,' writes Willingham, 'thinking is slow, effortful, and uncertain' (2010, p. 5). Being asked to focus, to learn, for many hours a day, for week after week and year after year (with homework thrown in, as well as summative and formative tests) is hugely demanding for pupils and their teachers.

There are commentators who yearn for an 'irresistible' school experience. For example, Tim Brighouse and Mick Waters say:

'We have to address the irreconcilable expectations and images which date from Victorian times that schooling is something to survive and suffer; we still reward pupils and punish them with a 'release' from the burden of schooling. We need to create a school experience that is irresistible, with learning that pupils don't want to turn away from because it is intrinsically absorbing and valuable in the widest possible sense, however challenging and demanding it may be. To miss a day of schooling should be a disappointment.' (2022, p. 598)

In such a world, Shakespeare's universal 'whining schoolboy… creeping like snail/ Unwillingly to school' would be a thing of the past. Can this be achieved? And, if so, how? Like a lesson plan and a scheme of work, it is perhaps in the detail where the learning can be seen. The school leaders we talked to have thought in great depth, and with imagination, about what they can teach, how they can teach it and how it can be assessed. They were asked to consider what they felt the ideal curriculum would look like, what role assessment should play in the taught curriculum, and their opinion on whether or not that assessment works.

Ballarat Clarendon College

Fact file

Number of pupils: 1,875

Age range: 3–18

Co-educational/Single sex: Co-educational

Location: Australia

State-funded/Independent: Independent

When was it established? 1864 (as Ballarat College, a boys' school). It later merged with Clarendon Presbyterian Ladies College.

Head/Contributor: Head: David Shepherd (Principal); Contributor: Greg Ashman (Deputy Principal)

Our pupils come from: Ballarat, Country Victoria and Melbourne, with a few from overseas and interstate.

Our values: Learning, effort, responsibility, community and wellbeing.

Our focus statement: Throughout a student's time at Ballarat Clarendon College our focus is to maximise their competence, skills and capacity so that, at the end of their time at the school, when they stand on the threshold of their future, they can pursue their heart's desire.

Our academic and pastoral vision: We do not have separate academic and pastoral visions. Both work together, informed by our focus statement. Note that a student's heart's desire may involve giving back to the community, leadership or simply being the best friend they can be. Every experience is an opportunity for learning.

In the future: We have a strategic plan to collaborate with others, learn from them and share what we have learnt.

Is there such a thing as the perfect curriculum?

I am not sure I am in a position to say. I can only talk about what we do. The central spine of our curriculum is English, mathematics, history and science. These encapsulate distinct ways of knowing about the world that we wish students to appreciate. In addition, we teach performing arts, visual arts, physical education, languages, humanities such as global politics and economics, accounting, legal studies, health and wellbeing.

In addition, our Year 9 (UK Year 10) students complete an eight-week experiential learning programme at our Yuulong campus which, through hikes, cooking, learning to surf and other activities, moves them out of their comfort zone in a controlled and safe environment.

Our curriculum is knowledge-rich. After reviewing the evidence, we are unconvinced of the existence of general purpose skills, such as critical thinking or creativity. Instead, we see these as functions of expertise in different subject areas. They still must be deliberately cultivated, but creativity in art will not affect creativity in mathematics.

Our knowledge-rich curriculum provides students with mental resources they may apply to a range of situations, both at school and in their wider lives. Knowledge is what we think *with*. We view long-term memory not as a library where we look up facts, but as a box of many specialised tools that comprise our human superpower – the ability to pick up where others left off and not have to invent every solution for ourselves.

What role should assessments play in the taught curriculum?

We use assessment mainly formatively. If you visited our school, the first thing you would be likely to notice is the highly interactive nature of the lessons, with students providing answers to the teacher every few minutes on mini-whiteboards or via turn-and-talk activities.

We also have a system of 'Phase II' meetings. After each formal assessment, we look at between-class data on a question-by-question basis. Given that we have all used the same lesson materials and tasks, we have a chance of identifying the one thing a teacher may have done that helped their students achieve more on a question than students in other classes. Once we have identified this, we write it into the curriculum for next year and we add it to our review and/or spaced practice programme.

We use a mix of continuous assessment and exams. We don't believe any exam is 'high stakes' until the final VCE (Victorian Certificate of Education) exams that students sit at the end of Year 12. Note that there is no equivalent of GCSEs in Australia, i.e. there are no state or national exams at age 16. We do have National Assessment Program Literacy and Numeracy (NAPLN) assessments of literacy and numeracy in Years 3, 5, 7 and 9, but we do not consider these to be high stakes.

How do you know your curriculum works?

We draw on research evidence. In fact, part of my role is to ensure we are informed by the best available research evidence. Unfortunately, a lot of education research is of poor quality. New initiatives are tested against business as usual, if there is any control group at all, and placebo effects are misunderstood as demonstrating the effectiveness of the programme. We therefore tend to zoom in to smaller-scale cognitive science studies (such as those demonstrating the effectiveness of retrieval practice) and zoom out to larger-scale correlational studies (such as the process-product research of the 1960s which attempted to get teachers to adopt behaviours of more effective teachers). Although we cannot be sure this is the cause, as we have implemented more and more of this research evidence our NAPLAN results have improved to be either above or well above those achieved by similar students [at other schools], and our VCE results have seen us top the state.

We do have an individualised curriculum, but through necessity. There is no off-the-shelf, knowledge-rich curriculum we could draw upon. The Australian curriculum is an extremely thin syllabus document so, although we follow that, it is nowhere near enough in scope or depth. We have an extensive co-curricular programme that includes traditional sports, rowing – which is big in Ballarat – and performing arts, alongside community initiatives such as 'food is free'. We see all as opportunities for learning.

As for the future? Well, there will be no revolutions. We follow an iterative approach.

Bedales

Fact file

Number of pupils: 800

Age range: 3–18

Co-educational/Single sex: Co-educational

Location: UK

State-funded/Independent: Independent

When was it established? 1893

Head/Contributor: Will Goldsmith

Our pupils come from: Hampshire in the pre-prep and prep, then more London, the south-east of England and the world.

Our values: Progressive and liberal, not for the sake of being different, but because we believe it is important for a properly rounded and relevant education. We also believe in the value of creativity for all young people in every aspect of their learning, not just in the 'creative' subjects.

Our academic vision: Bedales aims to be a progressive liberal education based on our communitarian 'work of each for weal of all' principle that develops creative, critically thinking life-long learners.

Our pastoral vision: Anticipating adult life, valuing the individual, with mutual respect at its cornerstone.

Is there such a thing as the perfect curriculum?

Schools should be free to teach what teachers think is best for their students in their context, informed by a broad set of national guidance but free of overly centralised and controlling government diktat. We are guided by thinking about educating the head, the heart and the hand. Assessment should inform and not dictate what is taught, with a variety of forms of assessment and only a leaving certificate (adaptable to the needs of individual students) that is made up of a portfolio of qualifications.

Our Bedales Assessed Courses (BACs) are a real strength, currently replacing GCSEs in 14 subjects, approximately 50% of our offering up to age 16. Subjects include digital game design, global awareness and outdoor work. We also have an exciting enrichment curriculum at sixth form and learning further down the school that is informed by our globally minded and environmental values. Students regularly learn about sustainability, the environment, food, craft and farming in our outdoor work curriculum that is unique to Bedales, based around the seasonal cycles and running of the school farm.

Rather than 'weaknesses', we are focusing on improving our wellbeing, environmental and technological curricula, mapping out a 'learning journey' from ages 3 to 18 in these areas to better meet the needs of the current time and the future. This will be accompanied by the development of a student's individual digital portfolio, which will stay with them throughout their schooling and provide rich and varied testimony of their learning.

What role should assessments play in the taught curriculum?

We use assessment as much as possible for learning as well as continually allowing students and teachers to understand where they are in their work. We have been teaching our BACs for the past 17 years and the number of subjects that have moved over from GCSEs to BACs has grown. In the future, we hope to increase this number even further, to give our students even greater freedom and flexibility, as well as preparing them better for A level studies in all subjects.

On a regular cycle, we undertake 'reviews' of each year group where we analyse every student's attainment and effort, deciding on individualised responses to each young person in our school to ensure that, going forward, they continue to grow and develop. Fundamental to their success is the deep understanding of the learners in and out of the classroom. The emphasis on relationships in everything we do at Bedales is particularly useful with assessment – by removing unnecessary hierarchies, we are better placed to see the whole person in every aspect of their growth.

There is definitely a place for all forms of assessment, including high-stakes final examinations. However, the current balance in the English system is directed way too far towards the latter. While grade inflation was definitely a problem, the solution should not simply be to eradicate virtually all other forms of assessment. Students taking our BACs are assessed throughout their courses, using a range of methods including logs, presentations, group project work, extended essays and the making of artefacts. The ubiquity of AI is an opportunity to ask what we value when we assess students. If a computer program can write essays, what *human* qualities do we value and therefore want to assess: curiosity, creativity, compassion? We are actively exploring how to assess in innovative ways, whether that is through project-based learning or creating 'escape rooms' in philosophy, religion and ethics.

If teachers were sufficiently skilled and empowered with broad guidelines then, in an ideal world, every student would be allowed to explore their passions and determine when they were ready for assessments. The practical consequences of institutionalising education means that it is currently impractical. Furthermore, government desire to scrutinise, compare and control has meant a narrowing of curricula and assessment.

How do you know your curriculum works?

Our students have a proven track record in success at higher education level, with the top two destinations last summer being Edinburgh and Bristol Universities. Our students go on to the most selective institutions in the UK and abroad – including both the traditionally 'academic' and also art/music courses – and they tend to stick to their courses more than their counterparts from other UK independent schools.

We use MidYIS and Alis (two school management systems) to track student progress, as well as the usual internal data on key assessments. Research by Harvard Education has also provided external validation for our approach to teaching and learning.

The 'taught curriculum' extends into the 'extra-curricular' in that what we do on the sports pitches, on the farm, in the theatre or the concert hall are also 'taught'. We define the 'extra' as 'co-curricular' to ensure that sufficient emphasis is placed on multiple forms of learning and not just 'academic' learning in classrooms. Some of the most powerful, useful and enduring lessons take place outside of conventional learning spaces and we make sure all of our students make the most of every part of what we have to offer.

There is potentially a big difference between where the curriculum and assessments will be in five years' time for the nation, the world and Bedales. We have been creating our own courses for 16 years and are therefore somewhat further ahead of the rest of the sector in terms of innovating our curriculum. We are fortunate to have that freedom and be able to exercise our independence from the state system in England, at least in part, and we intend to expand that freedom further in the future. We hope to be teaching our own curriculum up to 16, in the sciences and modern foreign languages, alongside our existing BACs, deploying a wider range of modes of assessment and controlling the content of our curriculum more. We also hope to have at least started looking at our sixth form offer by that stage too.

Green School Bali

Fact file

Number of pupils: approximately 450

Age range: 3–18

Co-educational/Single sex: Co-educational

Location: Indonesia

State-funded/Independent: Independent

When was it established? 2008

Head/Contributor: Leslie Medema (Head of campus)

Our pupils come from: All over the world.

Our values: iRespect (**i**ntegrity, **r**esponsibility, **e**quality, **s**ustainability, **p**eace, **e**mpathy, **c**ommunity and **t**rust). At all times, we are teaching and modelling these values and supporting our students in doing the same. We encourage all teachers to honour and recognise these values in our students with ongoing dialogue, discussions and reinforcement.

Our academic vision: To pioneer education for a sustainable future.

Our pastoral vision: To nurture a sense of passion and purpose in our students, so they can go on to make a positive difference in the world and for the world.

In the future: Education has to change. There is no other option. What is happening with our environment and with climate change will be the defining challenge for young people today and future generations to come. Educating for a sustainable future is now a need to have, not a nice to have.

Is there such a thing as the perfect curriculum?

When it comes to our curriculum, our students co-create their learning journey alongside teachers. What that means is they are empowered to share their passions, to express the things they are curious about and to seek answers to those questions. By doing this, we communicate to our students that their opinions matter, their way of being in the world and thinking about the world matters; it is honoured and respected. They develop a love of learning that continues long after leaving Green School and will serve them for years to come, in a world where the only constant is rapid change and innovation.

We go beyond 'green studies' or 'environmental studies' being a topic that stands separate from the rest of the curriculum. Rather, we plan everything through the lens of sustainability, using tools such as the Sustainability Compass which looks at nature, wellbeing, society and economy; as well as integrating the United Nations' Sustainable Development Goals and Permaculture principles. Most importantly, our curriculum is experienced. This is the part of the Green School's magic that is very hard to define, yet found everywhere on campus. From the 'Liquid Gold' (compost) mined from the worm farms in lower primary, to the impact of our service trips into the forests of Kalimantan in high school. These are experiences that impact students' lives beyond measure, and are a product of a flexible and 'living' curriculum.

Our schools and curriculum are living things, nothing is set in stone here. This, in itself, is a challenge. As we [personally] grow and evolve, we can make changes. As our world grows and evolves we can make changes. The challenge there is it puts an extra burden on educators to constantly come up with new and relevant ideas, activities and lesson plans rather than using one standardised template. Because of this, we are challenged to find educators who are extremely passionate and aligned with our mission and vision – then we have to convince them to move to Bali! Which, I suppose, is not all that difficult thankfully! From day one, we have been on such an incredible learning journey with our Green School community, and the journey is what life is all about.

We will never have a standardised curriculum because it goes against the concept of a living curriculum that is foundational to a Green School. However, as we expand with new Green Schools around the world, we provide educational frameworks to guide the learning programme, while still affording the flexibility it needs to innovate as the world changes, as well as localising the experiential aspect to the opportunities and problems unique to that community and cultural context.

What role should assessments play in the taught curriculum?

Our students are assessed holistically and based on their individual skills and passions. We use any type of assessment activity or assessment tool (including self-assessments). They are not dictated by standardised exams.

Every child's learning journey is unique to them and thus, they have opportunities to incorporate experiences with music, sport, community volunteering and more into their schooling. That said, we also have Model UN, a student leadership association, surfing, volleyball, a science lab and many other activities available to students after school, where they can continue to pursue passions while nurturing their lifelong love of learning.

How do you know your curriculum works?

Apart from our many fantastic alumni who have gone on to do incredible and impactful things in the world, our school and curriculum has been recognised by the World Economic Forum, named the Greenest School on Earth and just last year was a finalist for the World's Best School Prize.

Our parents want to go to Green School too! So much so, in fact, that schools have dedicated parent co-working and communing buildings on campus, where they can gather for coffee, attend presentations from educational experts, authors, climate activists and more, learn from workshops about sustainable living, [such as] how to DIY your own cleaning supplies or beauty products, and so much more. It's actually [an] essential part of a child's holistic development [i.e.] that their parents are learning alongside them and putting the values we emphasise at school into practice at home.

As for the future, I honestly couldn't say, because as mentioned we have such a living curriculum that – much like the world in which we live – nothing stays the same. I would love to see education shake off outdated student assessment practices that are often mired in systems of inequality and oppression and don't account for diversity of learning styles, socio-economic backgrounds, etc. Instead, we need to look at the whole student – understand where they are coming from and what resources they have had access to before comparing apples to oranges and putting exacting and unfair standards on them. A student who has a family that can provide them with three square meals a day, a tutor to help with standardised testing, and free time to take extra-curriculars in music, sport and so on, should not be assessed by the same standard as a student who has had to work two jobs on top of school and is helping care for younger siblings with limited access to food and nutrition. There are so many young people today with so much to offer our world, if only we'd take the time to really meet them where they are, understand them and encourage them.

International School of Geneva

Fact file

Number of pupils: 4,400

Age range: 3–18

Co-educational/Single sex: Co-educational

Location: Switzerland

State-funded/Independent: Independent

When was it established? 1924, the world's first international school (notwithstanding some debate about what the term 'international school' means).

Head/Contributor: Conrad Hughes (Director General)

Our pupils come from: Over 130 nationalities, making us by far the world's most diverse school (in terms of student nationalities).

Our values: Education for peace, the nourishing of global competences, international mindedness, inclusion, diversity, equity, anti-racism, bilingualism.

Our focus statement: Educating global citizens with the courage and capacity to create a just and joyful tomorrow together.

Our academic vision: This is best expressed in the Learner Passport, a transcript that captures learning wherever it has happened in both academic and extra-curricular domains, described through the lens of global competences. In partnership with UNESCO's International Bureau of Education, the seven global competences that we have identified as areas for human flourishing are: lifelong learning, self-agency, interacting with the world, interacting with others, interacting with diverse tools and resources, transdisciplinarity and multi-literateness.

Our pastoral vision: Mentors engage with students in a series of one-on-one conversations. These serve as check-ins and use the principles of life coaching to bring out student interests, challenges, goals and potential issues, always with the central notion that students have the keys to unlock any problems they might be facing. Fundamentally, we wish to build resilience in our students to face life's challenges with inner strength, confidence and humanity.

Is there such a thing as the perfect curriculum?

A perfect curriculum is a rich, inclusive curriculum that allows for different strengths to be recognised. I believe that it is important to offer students a broad curriculum for them to have some grounding in the different dimensions of the human story and not to be narrowly specialised too early on.

We were one of the schools to develop the International Baccalaureate Diploma Programme in the late 1960s, and to this day, it is the one diploma that all campuses offer. I think that two tremendous strengths of the programme are theory of knowledge (a course in epistemology that all students follow) and CAS (an acronym for creativity, activity and service, meaning that all students must engage in something creative, something active and some form of community service). A weakness of a broad-based curriculum is that it is very demanding, possibly more so than a narrow curriculum and, as such, it asks a lot of students, sometimes too much.

What role should assessments play in the taught curriculum?

We've had Dylan Wiliam run training sessions with us to focus on the essentials of embedded formative assessment; quality feedback, ongoing checking for understanding, clear assessment purpose and focussing on the learning rather than the teaching. It's project-based learning essentially. In our Universal Learning Programme, run on one of our campuses through a partnership with UNESCO, students do character projects, passion projects and mastery projects. The advantage of these is that learning is deep, ongoing and authentic. High-stakes assessments tend to test performance rather than deep understanding.

How do you know your curriculum works?

Assessment choice is more of an ideological and normative phenomenon than an empirical/evidence-based one. It's not easy to prove that one form of testing is better than another. Quality depends less on assessment form and more on assessment design (irrespective of the type of assessment) and the quality of the people rating it. Whether assessment form choice is fit for purpose or not simply depends on what you are looking for. I like projects because they show a journey and allow for some student freedom and exploration.

Ultimately, each school should have an individualised curriculum, because the more freedom you give schools and teachers, the more passion and intentionality, creativity and professional engagement you will get. Treating schools as examination centres and teachers as standardised test preppers does not really engage their true potential. Human talent grows best when you work with what you've got, rather than trying to make everybody the same. However, I still think it's important to have some core elements of the curriculum shared across syllabi, in order to create a broader sense of identity and affiliation.

Fortunately, we have a marvellous parent body that loves the school and stands by our values. In fact, we run an event called the 'parents promoting pedagogy' through which parents address the community on themes that they are passionate about. Schools are not just about students and teachers, they are about involving parents in the dialogue of education too.

In the future, hopefully our Learner Passport will have influenced many more schools and universities across the globe, allowing for assessment to be more inclusive. The Learner Passport recognises extra-curricular activities with the same validity and appreciation as academic subjects. A student who does remarkable work in sustainability will be eligible for competence recognition in 'interacting with the world', alongside a student who scores highly in the humanities.

Reach Academy Feltham

***

Fact file

Number of pupils: approximately 920

Age range: 2–18

Co-educational/Single sex: Co-educational

Location: UK

State-funded/Independent: State-funded

When was it established? 2012

Head/Contributor: Matilda Browne (Primary Co-Headteacher)

Our pupils come from: Our school is based in Feltham, a diverse part of west London. 43.6% of our pupils are eligible for the pupil premium and 53.6% have English as an additional language. 3% of our student population have educational health care plans with an additional 14.7% on the SEN register.

Our values: Reflect, endeavour, aspire, show courage and have fun (an acronym for Reach).

Our academic vision: For all children to gain the skills, attributes and academic qualifications to go on and live a life of choice and opportunity. We bring this vision to life every day and know that in order to have pupils leaving us at 18 ready to live out this vision we must develop the whole child. We know that academically, qualifications and skills matter when it comes to the next steps in life. We have very high aspirations for all of the pupils at our school and have high standards for our teachers to ensure that they are delivering the highest level of instruction every day.

Our pastoral vision: We pride ourselves on our pastoral work with pupils. We are a small school, with only 60 children per year group, which enables us to build a depth of relationship with both the pupil and their family. We work in partnership with parents and carers and we believe that this is vital if pupils are going to reach the highest standards of success. We balance our academic rigour with a broad variety of enrichment opportunities, from annual residentials to sports fixtures to after school clubs.

Is there such a thing as the perfect curriculum?

The ideal taught curriculum for schools starts with an aspirational end in mind. It then works back from that point to ensure that, throughout their education, pupils are hitting key targets on their journey to academic success at A level. At Reach, we refer to this as our 'backwards planned curriculum', the first principle of our curriculum design. An ideal taught curriculum is broader than any exam specification and truly considers what knowledge is key for pupils to go on to live successful lives in the future. Key knowledge needs to be embedded throughout the curriculum, regularly revisited and durably applied throughout a student's studies. The resources through which a curriculum is delivered are also vital if the intended curriculum is to be enacted with fidelity by every teacher in the school, thereby ensuring an equity of experience for all. Pupils must see themselves in the curriculum, and therefore the diversity and inclusivity of its content should consistently be reviewed, revised and revisited. The ideal taught curriculum is never complete but rather it is an iterative process and constantly subject to review. This can be based on pupil outcomes that should be measured regularly and effectively, but also feedback from staff and pupils should be sought, to ensure that the curriculum continues to stay true to the principles mentioned above.

As our first Reception cohort enters Year 11, we can see the strength in our backwards planned curriculum, which has mapped their academic journey in our school since September 2012. The strength and flexibility of their knowledge is a testament to this, as is their willingness and ability to express this, alongside their own opinions, both in written and spoken word. Our curriculum materials, particularly in humanities and science where booklets are used, lend themselves to successful enactment of the intended curriculum, and this enables even inexperienced teachers to teach effectively, as demonstrated by pupil outcomes. We have a strong focus in primary on reading, through highly effective early phonics teaching, which develops fluency into carefully selected comprehension of key texts. We can see the impact of this throughout the rest of our curriculum where pupils' reading ability supports them in many other subjects.

It is vital that we continuously review our curriculum through the lens of diversity, equity and inclusion. We want pupils to see themselves represented in our curriculum and have undertaken a larger piece of work around this in school, greatly supported by pupil voice. We are also working on feedback. It is vitally important that pupils can articulate their learning and are clear on their next steps. In order to achieve this, all pupils need to be given regular, timely feedback which helps them to improve.

What role should assessments play in the taught curriculum?

There is a clear challenge in measuring progress from 2–18 years old. Children pass through a number of different examination systems in this period and it has certainly been a challenge to have one clear view of assessment which works for all. We have decided that it is most appropriate to track key learning onto the primary grade boundaries (working towards, 'expected', 'standard' and 'greater depth') at this level, as opposed to starting them on the GCSE 1–9 grading scale. The other key change is creating an appropriate flight path that reduces the focus on key exam years, but rather ensures a cohort's clear progression in every year, instead of just at crunch points when there are external examinations. This is currently being benchmarked from Year 1 data in the autumn term, from which we track the cohort's path to have 0% 'working towards', 40% 'expected standard' and 60% 'greater depth'. This is based on the number of pupils and therefore each teacher knows at the start of each year how many need to move up a certain band.

We do low-stakes quizzing throughout a unit of work. This regular retrieval is based on the principles of cognitive science and ensures that pupils are learning more and remembering more; encoding new knowledge securely into pre-existing schemas. These quiz scores are recorded but are not reported to parents. We also do this in less-formal settings; for example, in Reception upwards, we pose questions about prior learning at lunch time. This could be anything from: 'How many genres of music can you name?' to 'What is your favourite dinosaur and why?' Three times a year, we have summative assessment points from Year 1 upwards. These are recorded, analysed and reported to parents. This ensures that we are keeping track of all pupils' progress, but particularly those in vulnerable groups, including pupil premium and SEN.

How do you know your curriculum works?

The first evidence source is our comparison to national data, particularly given the context of our school. We exceed the national average at every data point, from 98% of our Year 1 pupils passing the phonics screen in 2022 (the national average was 75%), to a progress 8 score of 0.83 in the same year (the national average was −0.03). However, we also gather evidence on a more regular basis. One important element of this is pupil voice. We want to ensure that pupils are remembering key knowledge and are able to talk about this and apply it to new contexts.

If we have totally individualised curricula, then some pupils might miss out, which can isolate them in their future lives. This could be anything from Shakespeare to the weather cycle; knowledge of both of these things are key to being a learned human being. This matters as powerful knowledge opens doors, and often those experiencing the most disadvantage are the ones who miss out, if this is not taught in all schools. I always refer to the example of the book *Dear Zoo*, regularly read in Early Years settings. It is a great book, but quite inaccessible if you have never been to an actual zoo! However, this does not mean that we should not aim to support our pupils to identify themselves in the curriculum. A good example of this is the absence of any reference to non-White soldiers in many history units about World War 1, or a lack of study of the African Kingdoms as an example of the historical concept of Empire. A Ukrainian pupil at our school recently told me that, until the recent war, no one knew anything about his country. This is a problem! This is not the binary 'Stormzy versus Shakespeare' argument but, rather, a considered approach to curricula. One that understands that there is a powerful body of concepts and knowledge that pupils should learn, but looks beyond the traditional remit of how these have previously been taught.

Curriculum is an iterative process and I hope that in five years' time ours will be even better. I hope that it will be supporting pupils to gain even better outcomes, for 100% to gain 5 A*–C at A level. I hope it will continue to become more representative of our school community and informed by the voices of our own pupils. I hope that the resources will continue to develop to support teacher delivery to be even more effective, so that our curriculum works for our most vulnerable and truly ensures success for all, enabling every child to go on to live a life of choice and opportunity.

Another view

This section presents the personal perspective of Dale Bassett, whose background in exam-board curriculum design focuses on a perhaps more 'traditional' way of thinking about curriculum, exams and assessment from that of our contributors, i.e. that the focus of any curriculum should be centred around the teaching of basic academic knowledge, which results in essential core learning. He takes the view that while there is a place for an evolving curriculum that embraces today's societal demands, this should not be to the detriment of 'traditional' knowledge acquisition.

Dale Bassett, non-executive director and trustee of several educational organisations and a former director at Assessment and Qualification Alliance (AQA). He writes here in a personal capacity.

Should curriculum change over time? A moment's consideration suggests that it must. Today's young people need to learn how to navigate a bewildering array of personal finance products. Climate change is an existential, global challenge. The rapidly-evolving knowledge economy has different skills demands, compared to the industries of the past.

These new challenges bring demands for radical curriculum change. However, the fundamental knowledge and skills that today's young people need have not, in fact, substantially changed. Of course, there are fast-moving, important disciplines like computer science that had to be brought into the curriculum. But most of the same core knowledge and skills are as important today as ever.

'Traditional' academic disciplines remain essential: lessons in personal finance are a lot less valuable if pupils' maths skills aren't good enough for them to understand concepts like compound interest. Swathes of science and geography can be taught through the lens of climate change. The greater emphasis needed on modern workplace skills, such as collaboration, is often best met through effective teaching rather than acting as a replacement for subject content.

We know that a broad range of knowledge is important to equip young people with the 'cultural capital' they will need to thrive (Hirsch, 1988). Once considered a traditionalist view, now every excellent school seeks to do this, particularly those serving more disadvantaged pupils, for whom it can be especially important.

Putting 'traditional' academic knowledge at the heart of the curriculum is not a utilitarian, exam-focused or narrowing approach. Quite the opposite: a broad curriculum is important, as acknowledged by everyone from Ofsted (2019), to campaigners such as the National Baccalaureate Trust (www.nationalbacctrust. org), of which this author is a trustee.

Above all, we are fortunate to have a strong evidence base to understand what makes an effective curriculum, with a wealth of research showing 'what works'. Willingham and others have shown that knowledge is important for learning itself, since the more knowledge readers have about the topic of a text, the better they will understand it (Willingham, 2012; Lipson and Cooper, 2002).

In curriculum design, 'big ideas' are essential to ensure that pupils develop conceptual understanding and don't just learn 'facts' to be regurgitated in an exam (Scheerens and Bosker, 1997). Sequencing of the curriculum is also key to effective learning (Ofsted, 2019): a well-planned curriculum, taking account of the wealth of research about how we learn, may use techniques such as spaced practice [in which learning, rather than being concentrated into long, intense periods is in distributed, shorter bursts] (Rohrer and Taylor, 2006; Rawson and Kintsch, 2005), interleaving (Richland et al., 2005; Rohrer et al., 2015) and retrieval practice (Barenberg et al., 2018; Roediger and Karpicke, 2006) to optimise learning.

Of course, curricula should evolve over time – but with evidence, and thus stability, at its core.

Reflections

How can assessment be used effectively to embed and extend learning?

The contributors in this chapter have asked themselves such a question and tried to find workable solutions. Ballarat Clarendon College in Australia has a national curriculum which is, according to Greg Ashman, 'extremely thin'. This allows them to develop a knowledge-rich curriculum, which places skills as functions of the expertise gained from having excellent subject knowledge. Progress is assessed through continuous assessment and examinations. This flexibility is also, although perhaps to a lesser extent, found in Bedales. This is another fee-paying school which uses its independence to build around the national curriculum. Ideally, for Will Goldsmith from Bedales, every student would be allowed to follow their passions. But, as he notes, how would teachers be trained to support this, and how could it be assessed? Matilda Browne from Reach Academy suggests that there are challenges in allowing schools too much freedom over what they teach and that if pupils miss out on foundational learning that can lead to difficulties in their future lives.

For some teachers, assessments usually mean standardised tests, and many see these as blunt, reductive tools that, arguably, measure attainment but do not empower learning. Teachers might see assessments as fixed, rather than the 'living things' that Green School Bali seeks so passionately to promote. Leslie Medema's students are assessed holistically and individually. It is a freedom that will be envied by many because, to a great extent, most schools are constrained by the requirements of the local district or the national government. Adherents of Assessment for Learning (AfL) advocate for this flexibility by encouraging the use of formative assessment. They argue that this employs students' learning to influence teaching to meet students' ongoing needs. The idea, promoted by Dylan Wiliam, became popular in schools around the world at the beginning of this century (and we can see its ongoing influence in this chapter at the International School of Geneva). The educationalist and author Tom Sherrington has commented, perhaps with some sense of exaggeration, that 'time was when you couldn't get a job unless you said "AfL" about 12 times in an interview' (Sherrington, 2019). Professor Robert Coe has gone so far as to say that 'it is now a rare thing… to meet any teacher in any school in England who would not claim to be doing Assessment for Learning' (Coe, 2013, p. 10). Wiliam condensed his ideas into five AfL strategies that could be used in the classroom (Wiliam and Thompson, 2008). They are: understanding learning intentions; arranging activities that show evidence of learning; providing feedback; students learning from one another; and students owning their own learning.

None of these ideas are original to AfL, but bringing them together into one clear approach has been highly effective for some schools. But, influential though AfL is thought to be, it has not revolutionised all schools. Coe has written that 'despite its near universal adoption and strong research evidence of substantial impact on attainment, there has been no (or, at best, limited) effect on learning outcomes nationally' (2013, p. 10). Even when teachers change the way they teach to try to move away from focusing on high-stakes tests, or try to eschew an over-reliance on a prescribed curriculum, the results may, unintentionally, be counterproductive. As Daisy Christodoulou, Director of Education at 'No More Marking' has observed about AfL: '... in the worst cases it actually ended up encouraging "teaching to the test" and over-frequent grading... because ... the value of exam tasks was overestimated, and other types of assessments were undervalued' (Christodoulou, 2017, p. 15).

Tom Richmond and Eleanor Regan from the EDSK think tank have published an evaluation of alternatives to examinations. Their research suggests that all forms of assessments have innate weaknesses, as well as strengths. They conclude by stating that 'the alternatives to exams explored... generally fare worse than exams in terms of their ability to differentiate between students in a precise and consistent manner' (Richmond and Regan, 2023, p. 64).

The recent COVID-19 pandemic gave all educators, around the world, the unprecedented opportunity to try teacher-assessed grades. However, there were challenges with this approach reported as well, including increased teacher workload and possible grade inflation (see Sherrington, 2021). The Sutton Trust claimed that teacher-assessed grades 'compounded existing inequalities', with children from disadvantaged backgrounds and Black children doing particularly badly (cited in Richmond and Regan, 2023, p. 25). If changes are to be made to the curriculum, then it is essential to have an assessment model that is fair and equitable and the search for this perhaps continues.

Learning for what end?

The schools interviewed had a range of aspirations and visions for their curricula. Some focussed on opportunity for their pupils. For example, Ballarat Clarendon College's focus statement talks about equipping students to 'pursue their heart's desire' and Reach Academy's vision is of a life of choice and opportunity for each pupil. Perhaps along similar lines, Dale Bassett suggested that aims might include equipping a pupil to be able to navigate their personal finance as they become an adult. Does this mean that schools should chiefly prepare children for the world of work? *The Times* newspaper recently set up a commission to look at the future of schools and what they teach in England. The final report, which was the result of over a year of meetings and consultations involving leading educationalists, delivered an action plan that called for new skills to be taught to our children. Andreas Schleicher contributed his thoughts to the commission's report, and his statement (cited by The Times Education Commission, 2022) that 'the education of today is your economy tomorrow' captured its prevailing tone.

Ricardo Hausmann (2015), Professor of the Practice of International Political Economy at Harvard Kennedy School, has written however:

> 'Most of the skills that a labor force possesses were acquired on the job. What a society knows how to do is known mainly in its firms, not in its schools. At most modern firms, fewer than 15% of the positions are open for entry-level workers, meaning that employers demand something that the education system cannot – and is not expected – to provide.'

Professor of Economics at George Mason University, Bryan Caplan (2023), has written, 'learning is a good thing in itself, regardless of its economic impact. But such a view is far outside the Overton window' [the spectrum of public policy and views on social issues considered acceptable at a given time]. Such a view perhaps echoes Bedales' academic vision of creating life-long learners who desire to know more and remain curious. Briony Scott, an Australian headteacher, puts it like this:

> 'Education takes place in one context, but knowledge is about life. And even knowledge must bow to wisdom. Wisdom, an old-fashioned word in so many contexts, is what allows our young men and women to make good decisions and to live fulfilled and thriving lives. You can be knowledgeable yet not be kind. You can have all the skills, belong to a great school, be well-educated and even have enormous knowledge – but in the true spirit of academia, it is wisdom we seek to be truly fulfilled, to make good decisions, for the benefit of others.' (Scott, 2023, p. 34)

This view echoes the Bedales motto of 'Work of Each for Weal of All', which was also expressed by a number of other schools interviewed. The International School of Geneva's vision is about preparing pupils for citizenship and not just of one particular state but for global citizenship. Green School Bali's aims arguably take this vision even further, seeking to equip pupils to make a positive difference towards a sustainable future. This range of aims from different schools may not give one, conclusive answer but it can, we hope, provide inspiration and grounds for reflection for us all.

Chapter 6

Use of technology in schools

It is tempting to say that schools are living through a technology revolution. For many teachers, the pandemic accelerated the move from 'analogue' to 'digital' teaching and learning. With schools closed, teachers accessed their classes via Google Meet™, Microsoft Teams and Zoom. The more affluent schools were able to be creative and ambitious in what they offered: indeed, some independent schools managed to move concerts, plays, parents' meetings and even internal examinations online. Some initiatives, it seems, worked well, some didn't and, as with many things relating to education, success was probably still to a great extent reliant on the quality of the teaching and the students' willingness to learn, rather than the media used.

Many less affluent schools often did not have the equipment to move across to online teaching (BBC News, 2021); in addition, not all their staff were sufficiently trained and, more importantly, many of the families with whom they worked did not have a device at home with which to access lessons (or, very often, had just one device shared by several family members). The 'learning loss' was difficult to measure and is still being calculated, but it seems that younger children and disadvantaged children suffered the most in England, for example (Newton, 2021).

Writer and essayist William Gibson allegedly remarked that 'the future is already here – it's just not evenly distributed yet' (Kennedy, 2012); perhaps this is particularly true in schools when we look at how technology is used in them. The authors of the *Times Education Commission* (2022), who spent a year collecting evidence on the state of UK schools, were critical of a system they characterised as being a 'recognisably 19th-century school and university education system, facilitated by 20th-century technology'. The system is, for educator and historian Anthony Seldon (2022), 'embarrassingly unfit for purpose in the 21st century'. Sir Ian Livingstone (founder of the Livingstone Academy, who is interviewed for this chapter), would no doubt agree.

Seldon and Livingstone are not alone in claiming that the United Kingdom is falling behind in the race to equip our children with the skills they need for an increasingly virtual future. Sir Ian says in his book, *Hacking the Curriculum* (Livingstone and Saeed, 2016): 'the robots are coming… [and] there's no point in training our children like robots, if real robots are going to take their jobs!' Numerous companies, consultants and authors now offer schools advice on how they can use technology to improve teaching and learning. How can schools decide what to implement or change when it comes to technology, if anything at all? Is a book better or worse than a tablet at developing literacy? Do employers favour a particular approach? Are there considerations about technology that go beyond the workplace? Each of our interviewees has shared their responses to these sorts of questions and indeed one of the schools featured, The Waldorf School in the Silicon Valley, has decided to deliberately eschew the use of certain technologies.

Some children have access to the latest devices, but many do not. In London, it is possible to visit schools with world-class information communication technology (ICT) resources, and then to walk down the road to another school in the same postcode, but perhaps in another sector, and see a very different set of facilities.

Some school leaders are perhaps wary of embracing new technology just for the sake of it. Many schools have likely at one time or another invested in new technology that has not been successful or long-lasting. Perhaps the most famous example of where schools and tech companies partnered together happened in 2013. As documented in *WIRED* magazine (Lapowsky, 2015), the Los Angeles Unified School District (LAUSD), which educated around 700,000 students, decided to give each one of them an iPad®. Each tablet would come equipped with educational software from a multinational publishing and assessment company. It would cost $1.3 billion. It was hailed at the time as visionary and pioneering but is now considered to have failed. Reasons cited included a lack of training for teachers, unreliable connectivity across the district, poor planning and too much reliance on one device. *WIRED* magazine (Lapowsky, 2015) commented that it now looks like a 'spectacularly foolish' initiative. Another journalist also commented that the funds used to finance this programme would normally have been used to build and repair schools (Newcombe, 2015).

As a number of interviewees in this chapter argue, however, when technology companies work closely with schools the results can be impressive: the students can gain from new methods of learning that would have been impossible without the devices used, and the skills and knowledge of their teachers.

Between 2013 and 2017, Microsoft founder Bill Gates invested over $300m in personalised learning (Wexler, 2018). He's not alone among the tech billionaire community. Facebook founder Mark Zuckerberg and his wife Priscilla Chan are also keen supporters (and investors) in personalised learning that is facilitated through technology. However, Paul Emerich France, a long-term advocate of personalised learning, suggests that placing too much emphasis on technology can have a dehumanising effect (2018). In fact, even Zuckerberg and Chan's own charity states that 'when students experience strong teacher-student connections, they are more likely to feel more motivated and engaged in school, which is critical to student learning' (Chan Zuckerberg Initiative, 2022).

Steve Jobs, founder of Apple and arguably one of the most influential figures of the 21st century, said in 1996 that what was wrong with education 'cannot be fixed with technology. No amount of technology will make a dent'. Jobs concluded that 'It's a political problem. The problems are sociopolitical' (cited in Wolf, 1996).

Diane Ravitch, Research Professor of Education at New York University, says that 'there is still no solid evidence that students learn more, or better, when taught by a computer'. Ravitch also claims that other risks to using technology in the classroom include the threat to student privacy from technology; the potential for technology for assessment to introduce inconsistencies or be inaccurate; a rise in cyber charter (or virtual, online) schools; and the financial power that technology companies can have. Ravitch (2017) writes:

'The greatest fear of parents and teachers is that the tech industry wants to replace teachers with computers. They fear that the business leaders want to cut costs by replacing expensive humans with inexpensive machines, that never require health care or a pension. They believe that education requires human interaction. They prefer experience, wisdom, judgment, sensibility, sensitivity and compassion in the classroom to the cold, static excellence of a machine.

I agree with them.'

But Ravitch was writing in 2017, and much has happened since then, including, of course, the global pandemic. And it may be the case that since the pandemic those parental views have changed because, as we shall see from interviews in this chapter, for many children, technology could maintain a connection between them and their teachers. Similarly, for many children who find conventional in-class learning at times more challenging, the efficiency, singular focus and clarity of individualised, computer-based learning could be game-changing and liberating, as seen in our interview with Neill Oldham in this chapter.

Equally, clear efficiencies emerged from the widespread use of software packages like Teams, OneNote and Zoom. The possibilities of online, in-the-moment assessment to offer speedy, personalised and targeted responses to students was one striking benefit of enforced digitalisation. Those teachers fortunate enough to be able to rely on universal access amongst their pupils were also able to see, right away, what their pupils had learnt and not learnt, as they completed their homework tasks online. That visibility could inform lesson planning straight away. Lessons could be replanned and redesigned immediately, based on the students' grasp of the task, immediately evident online. The pace, the efficiency, the sheer practical and administrative benefits are hard to ignore.

The other great disruptor that has shot a digital bolt over the global educational bows since the pandemic is the onset of AI software. ChatGPT (Generative Pre-Trained Transformer) was launched in November 2022 (see OpenAI, 2022). Daisy Christodoulou's 'No More Marking' research platform is currently exploring the efficacy of ChatGPT in providing useful feedback for students. The answer in March 2023, based on the ChatGPT-3 model, was that 'it can't do it all that convincingly... yet' (Christodoulou, 2023). Reports that ChatGPT has successfully passed the American bar exams (not just passed them, but aced them – at the 88th percentile) are likely giving governments around the world pause for thought (Mauran, 2023). EDSK, a think tank in the UK, has advised that coursework will need to be radically rethought in the light of AI development; assessment will be much more focused on spoken submissions, for example, and written coursework looks unlikely to be able to survive (Richmond and Regan, 2023). The UK government has produced some guidance to schools addressing the impact of AI (DfE, 2023) and it is convening a group of experts to look at this.

Schools are having to ask tough (and perhaps urgent) questions about the way they assess their pupils and how they can accurately judge progress.

Have technological changes in teaching during the pandemic had a lasting impact on how schools operate and how teachers teach? Has it shown us the many strengths of technology or, conversely, has it shown us its many limitations? Are teachers more valued than ever before and tablets and laptops seen increasingly as distractions, or is the opposite true? The authors of the 2015 Organisation for Economic Cooperation and Development (OECD) report *Students, Computers and Learning: Making the Connection* commented, 'technology can amplify great teaching but great technology cannot replace poor teaching'.

This chapter explores these questions through the lens of schools who have embraced the possibility of technology wholeheartedly. The chapter invites interviewees to comment on what they see as being the strengths of technology in the classroom, how it supports pupils in class and in the wider community (including pupils who require assistive learning), and what the challenges might be moving forward in the future.

LEO Academy Trust

Fact file	
Number of pupils: 4,000+	
Age range: 4–18	
Co-educational/Single sex: Co-educational	
Location: UK	
State-funded/Independent: State-funded (academy)	
When was it established? 2015	
Head/Contributor: CEO, Phillip Hedger	

Our pupils come from: LEO Academy Trust is a multi-academy trust, consisting of nine schools and serving over 4,000 pupils, across a wide range of socio-economic backgrounds in south London and Surrey.

Our values: Perseverance, respect, imagination, dedication, encouragement. They sit alongside our mission which is: learning, excellence, opportunities.

Our academic and pastoral vision: LEO Academy Trust is committed to developing a family of great schools, where collaboration makes a real difference for children, staff and communities. The trust's commitment to being outstanding is delivered through great learning communities, excellence for all and endless opportunity. We are committed to ensuring that children are safe and enjoy learning and that everyone feels included, respected and valued. We offer an ambitious curriculum that develops pupils for the challenges of life. Staff potential is recognised and invested in and we make a difference to the communities we serve.

What do you think are the strengths of technology in the classroom?

We gain a huge range of benefits from our approach to technology, the most important, of course, being the wider range of opportunities, resources and access to learning that our children receive. In addition, our staff have found their workload for some tasks has been reduced, teaching is far more child-initiated, and technology has really helped us to develop the use of Michael Fullan's 6 Cs (creativity, character education, citizenship, communication, critical thinking and collaboration). [Michael Fullan is an author, speaker, and educational consultant.]

We consider technology to be a crucial part of our organisation at all levels. It is crucial for how we operate, communicate and function, and this is equally true in our teaching and in our learning. In order to provide the very best teaching and learning for every pupil, both pupils and staff regularly engage with technology, albeit in different ways, based on the different needs of the children.

There is no doubt that, from what we see within schools in the LEO Academy Trust, our pupils gain huge benefit from our use of and approach to technology. Many children feel that they are far more independent – they have access to a wide range of teacher-curated content that can enable them to make independent choices about how, what and when they learn. Furthermore, many of our children feel that the technology and, in particular, our approach to assistive technology, has enabled them to access learning in different ways. Children who may have difficulties with reading are able to use technology to help them break down tricky words, to hear them aloud, or to use tools such as visual dictionaries or a more traditional word-based dictionary.

One-to-one devices are an incredibly powerful tool and can enhance teaching and learning. However, as with any resource, the procurement and initial technical piece of work is only the beginning. In order for one-to-one to be impactful, it is about the wider staff CPD [Continuing Professional Development] and implementation of effective pedagogy in the school that is really crucial. I also think that one-to-one devices do require staff teams to remain strategic and stay focused on teaching and learning, ensuring that this is at the heart of [everything a school] does.

How does technology support pupils?

Evidence-based approaches are embedded in our approach to teaching and learning, but also in our approaches to technology adoption and implementation. Drawing on reliable, accurate and authentic research from sources such as the EEF (Education Endowment Foundation) has really helped us to ensure that the provision we're providing for our pupils reflects current academic and professional thinking. Most recently, the LEO Academy Trust has engaged with a wide range of organisations and professionals to consider the concept of PedTech [PedTech refers to the appropriate pedagogy, supported by effective technology – see Aubrey-Smith, 2021 for more information], ensuring that there is clear alignment between our pedagogical practice and how technology is amplifying this.

When we initially considered the use of one-to-one devices, we very much operated in the 'substitution' pillar of the SAMR (substitution, augmentation, modification and redefinition) model [the SAMR model has four pillars of digital transformation – see Jisc, 2022 for more information]; we were very much substituting digital technology for more traditional, paper-based instruction methods. As our confidence, understanding and competency have developed, we now find ourselves using technology in far greater and more impactful ways. Staff are regularly making carefully considered choices about technology, selecting when the appropriate time is to utilise this resource and when a different resource may be more beneficial. Teachers are able to offer a much wider range of teaching and learning opportunities and activities due to technology being able to provide a wider range than they would have [had access to] previously.

Technology and the wider community

Pupils and parents have been extremely supportive about our approach to teaching and learning. Never before have parents had access to their child's learning on a daily basis; children are able to go home and share real examples of their learning with those they live with. Furthermore, children have appreciated the independence that technology can provide, particularly in adaptive teaching, where teachers are able to provide children with open-ended tasks, allowing children to design individual, personalised outcomes.

We've received a wealth of support, challenge and feedback from friends and colleagues within the tech industry, specifically Google, Adobe, Nearpod, Doodle, Kaligo and SchoolOnline to name just a few. Not only have tech providers been instrumental in helping us onboard, configure and deploy technology, but also in the ongoing conversations around measuring impact, constantly tweaking and enhancing provision, as well as providing opportunities to showcase and share practice with the sector.

The challenges ahead

Like many schools and colleges globally, one challenge that we all continuously face is to ensure that our professional practice in all areas of school life is constantly adapting, tweaking and changing to ensure that it remains evidence-informed and fully meets the needs of the community we serve. In order to do this fully effectively, it is crucial that every school and college sufficiently allocates resources to ensure this aspect is maintained.

As with every approach in education, there are challenges as well as opportunities from our approach to technology. Working alongside staff, parents and senior leaders in our schools, we strive to overcome these challenges to ensure that children have access to quality teaching and learning opportunities, amplified by technology. It is widely recognised that inappropriate and excessive amounts of screen time can have an impact on children. Within the LEO Academy Trust, we work with pupils and parents to ensure that technology is being used appropriately and we always endeavour to maintain a healthy balance of online and offline activities. Furthermore, we support parents to have discussions with their children around appropriate screen time. In addition to supporting parents, at the LEO Academy Trust we are fully committed to supporting and empowering teachers to utilise technology to enhance the outcomes and opportunities that we are able to provide children. The Trust has a considerable training and CPD programme to ensure that every member of staff feels confident and able to utilise technology impactfully.

Highfurlong School

Fact file

Number of pupils: 110
Age range: 2–19

Co-educational/Single sex: Co-educational

Location: UK

State-funded/Independent: State-funded

When was it established? 2015

Head/Contributor: Neill Oldham

Our pupils come from: Blackpool, Wyre and Fylde Coast area. Highfurlong is a special school in Blackpool catering for pupils with a wide range of complex disabilities and medical needs. Highfurlong is located on the border of Blackpool and Lancashire, and has pupils who attend from both local authorities. Highfurlong is a four-time Ofsted 'Outstanding' school.

Our values: Inspire, challenge, believe.

Our academic and pastoral vision: We inspire the Highfurlong family to be the best that they can be. Our bespoke curriculum provides challenge in all areas of education and development for the pupils and we believe everyone can flourish in our warm and friendly school. The school's mission statement of 'Inspire, challenge, believe' outlines the high expectations and aspirations the school has for its pupils. Highfurlong was the only special school to be part of the EdTech Demonstrator Programme from 2020–2021 due to the way the school utilises assistive technology, not only for access to the curriculum but also for social engagement.

What do you think are the strengths of technology in the classroom?

The use of technology supports our students with additional needs to access education and to communicate in order to achieve their potential and to live a fulfilled life. By using technology, much of which is assistive technology, we can support our children and young people to reach their potential and open up avenues such as higher education and employment which, without the means to express themselves and the opportunity to show what they can do, would otherwise be unimaginable. Whilst we promote and believe in the use of technology to engage and support teaching and learning, we also believe that there is a time and a place for it. If technology doesn't enhance learning, then we won't use it. Students can definitely have technology fatigue, as can staff, and we see technology as one of many teaching tools. There are times when the pupil may not want to engage with technology and prefer a more practical learning opportunity; technology is not always the answer.

Using technology removes lots of barriers for our children. Rather than creating or typing a piece of work, allowing pupils to use voice notes can remove significant barriers. Utilising assistive technology provides our pupils with as much independence as possible and reduces that adult reliance, giving them skills they can transfer outside of school. Many of our pupils are unable to physically access conventional laptops or PCs and require specialist assistive technology. The students gain so much time from technology; using features such as dictation or word banks saves hours of typing out. We also see the confidence of our pupils increase with the use of technology. Allowing their work to be read back to them on screen, be it through the read aloud feature on Google Docs or from the reader pen during independent reading time, allows them to self-correct before submitting their work to the teacher.

How does technology support pupils?

Using technology allows us to gain a true understanding of our pupils' abilities. This supports our assessments, as our pupils have the means to record their work independently and communicate with us about what they understand. This, in turn, supports our lesson planning and delivery as teachers are then confident that they are pitching work at the right level, which can be very tricky to do when teaching phonics to a pupil who is non-verbal with complex health needs. The impact of having such a focus on technology for work output and communication is that we dedicate a lot of staff training hours to this, but we feel it is essential for our practice.

Technology has unlocked the potential in many pupils – with this in mind, we have had to go back to the foundations of our curriculum and ensure that we are providing the right level of breadth and challenge. We have gained invaluable insights into the likes and dislikes of pupils, what their interests are and indeed their future aspirations – we have used this to ensure that our curriculum and teaching fosters and develops these interests, so that pupils are prepared for the next stage in their education and beyond.

There are some additional vulnerabilities that our pupils face due to their learning needs and physical needs. We have to ensure that our pastoral care and our PSHE (including sex and relationships) teaching is appropriate for them and designed to keep them safe. Much of this includes targeted work around being safe online. Our relationship curriculum focuses on both physical contact and behaviours as well as digital interactions – looking at social media, images, consent and understanding digital footprints – what we post is there, can be shared and saved even if we delete it in the future.

Technology and the wider community

Since 2019 we have used Seesaw as our virtual learning environment. We had the majority of parents sign up and engage with it in its early stages, then through the pandemic those remaining families saw its potential and now we have a 99%

engagement rate with our families for sharing information between home and school. We also appreciate that some families prefer not to use technology, so we use other means of communication with them.

We have strong links with technology providers and they have delivered numerous training sessions to our staff. Based on our relationships with our tech suppliers and our experience with their after-purchase care, we are able to signpost other schools to them. We have done numerous external presentations with our suppliers, giving case studies of real experience with their products and our pupils.

The challenges ahead

Keeping up to date with ever-changing technology can be a challenge. In order to purchase wisely, you need to have an idea of the technology that's out there, and we encourage our staff to utilise the features to their full capacity with regards to the hardware and software we already have before looking to purchase something else. Maintaining and tracking the technology is a big aspect of using it in school; luckily we have a team that shares this responsibility. With any school, staff turnover is a challenge and that brings around new training needs with new starters. We have created a bank of training videos to support this and have built these training videos into our induction process.

The Glasgow Academy

Fact file

Number of pupils: 1,605 (800 students in the senior school and 805 students in the junior school)

Age range: 3–18

Co-educational/Single sex: Co-educational

Location: UK

State-funded/Independent: Independent

When was it established? 1845

Head/Contributor: Dr Matt Gibson (Head of Senior School)

Our pupils come from: The Glasgow Academy is principally located at Kelvinbridge, but also has two further sites in Milngavie and Newlands for Nursery, Kindergarten and Prep 1–4 pupils.

Our values: Service, endeavour, respect, valour and ambition.

Our academic vision: The school has a long tradition of fostering academic excellence. Results in external examinations are consistently among the best in the country.

Our pastoral vision: Our code is an agreed way of working and being amongst the school community to ensure that collectively all can flourish. We are committed to serving our Academy community. Through our work we aim to encourage all within this community to adopt this code. The code is summarised as: FIDEM. We are *fair* and transparent in all we do; we use *inclusive* practice and equality is demonstrated by embracing diversity and individuality and empowering all learners to be the best they can be; we are *dynamic* in our leadership, critically exploring and challenging attitudes, beliefs, assumptions, values and practices to improve professional and support pupils, staff and our wider community; we focus on *empowering* all learners through positive, professional and respectful relationships with learners, families, colleagues and other partners, buildng their capacity for leadership and their impact on their learning and wellbeing, and that of others; we concentrate on *motivating* and inspiring the people in our school community, building their capacity for leadership and their impact on their learning and wellbeing, and that of others.

What do you think are the strengths of technology in the classroom?

The education sector learnt a great deal through the accelerated adoption of technology in classrooms (or homes) during the COVID-19 pandemic. At The Glasgow Academy, we were acutely aware that many pupils could not connect to live lessons at the same time, as they were restricted by technology, by other responsibilities at home or, in some cases, by illness. We were also very aware that across the country the provision of live lessons was very limited. At a national level, this inequity of access was damaging for many young people and for the morale of staff across the sector too.

In the summer of 2020, a small team of educators at our school decided to try and help address this issue. Teaching is a surprisingly complex process. It requires a connection between humans – we learn best when we feel and experience something – and we recognised that this is often lost in the online space. We remember our most inspirational teachers for a reason: they elicited an emotional response as well as sharing knowledge. We wanted to try and find a way to bottle this kind of learning moment, but to do so at large scale, so it could be accessed flexibly and by large numbers of people and could be returned to again and again.

The team got to work with university academics, cognitive psychologists, ed-tech specialists and with feedback groups of pupils, parents and teachers to understand what was needed to bridge inspirational teaching with young people learning asynchronously online. The objective was to develop a media format and sharing platform that would allow access to returnable and shareable learning content; pushing learning into an online social space that included teachers and parents as well as students.

They aimed for low-tech, short-format content that did not lose the rich qualities of human communication. They collaborated with expert film-makers, retrained and upskilled their teachers, worked with communications coaches and applied advanced principles of cognitive science to make something new. They wanted to use digital technology to maximum effect by combining the knowledge of teachers, the science of learning and the art of communication.

Thinkfour is open access and free to use. There are no paywalls, no advertising, no data harvesting, no connections to big tech. It is simply a social impact initiative to bring the country's best teachers from lots of schools to the phones and tablets of every young person in the country. It does not seek to replace classroom teaching or real teachers. It simply uses what is currently the most significant power of technology – connectivity – to link people who want to learn, to those who can help them.

How does technology support pupils?

Establishing and maintaining this kind of project brings costs in both financial terms and staff time – in this regard there is an opportunity cost for other potential projects in a school environment. That said, there are no direct negative benefits for the school community. The pupils at this school, like all those in Scotland, benefit from an online learning resource that is specifically for their curriculum. In the longer term, it has developed a sustainable business model that ensures thinkfour can continue to make open-access content for anyone to benefit from.

Technology and the wider community

Our community is very proud of a project like this, not least because it goes well beyond our own school. It has served to identify The Glasgow Academy with having a 'bigger view', and an institutional and societal ambition which is a very attractive prospect for pupils and parents. It is also a clear responsibility for schools who are able to kickstart this kind of project to have an impact that benefits everyone.

The challenges ahead

The growth of technology has presented the thinkfour project with many opportunities. Many organisations seek to unlock institutional knowledge and to translate this into open-access content – we are now able to manage this process for them. Our challenge is to maintain the focus of our core mission – to share learning and to support the human process of teaching, without being distracted by the noise of unnecessary technology.

Livingstone Academy Bournemouth

> ### Fact file
>
> **Number of pupils:** 300 in Year 7 and 8 currently
>
> **Age range:** 7–18 (eventually)
>
> **Co-educational/Single sex:** Co-educational
>
> **Location:** UK
>
> **State-funded/Independent:** State-funded
>
> **When was it established?** 2021
>
> **Head/Contributor:** Sir Ian Livingstone (founder of the Livingstone Academy)
>
> **Our pupils come from:** Bournemouth and the local area
>
> **Our academic and pastoral vision:** The Livingstone Academy was set up in September 2021 by Sir Ian Livingstone (CBE) (along with the CEOs of Aspiration Academies Trust) as a school whose classrooms replicate the workplace as much as possible. Traditional, single-discipline learning sits alongside transdisciplinary assignment work, innovation and development weeks, project-based learning and presentation. The STEAM (science, technology, engineering, the arts and maths) curriculum is used as entry points to the rest of the curriculum. The Academy uses experiential, hands-on learning with a specific focus on gaming, as a means of embedding 21st-century skills and preparing pupils for the 21st-century workplace, whilst simultaneously delivering core elements of the national curriculum. We create an environment where our pupils can have raised aspirations, the skills necessary to be job creators as well as job seekers, and can achieve the best qualifications.

The strengths of technology

The power of play: I've been privileged to work in the UK's games industry for over four decades and I firmly believe that games are a contextual hub for learning.

I co-founded Games Workshop in 1975, launching *Dungeons & Dragons* in the UK and later *Warhammer,* both games being excellent for the imagination. In 1982, I co-wrote *The Warlock of Firetop Mountain*, the first interactive gamebook in the Fighting Fantasy series, which got a whole generation of children reading. These are books in which YOU, the reader, are the hero. Fighting Fantasy gamebooks are not like linear novels. They are branching narratives using numbered paragraphs to navigate the adventure – effectively analogue hypertext – with a game system attached, hence the term 'gamebook'. Set in worlds of monsters and magic, Fighting Fantasy gamebooks place the reader at the heart of the story, giving them agency over their own destiny. Choice is empowering. Children read and play through magical worlds of wonder, deciding which way to go, picking up clues, solving puzzles, finding treasure and rolling dice to slay monsters. Adding a games element to the branching narrative with multiple paths and endings makes the books exciting and compelling. Gamebooks are recognised as being excellent for reluctant readers, especially boys. Whilst enjoying Fighting Fantasy adventures readers are, at the same time, increasing their literacy, problem-solving, critical thinking and algorithmic thinking skills.

I moved into the video games industry in the 1990s and launched *Lara Croft: Tomb Raider*. Yes, playing games is fun and entertaining, but think about the cognitive process of what is happening when people play games. Playing a game requires problem-solving, decision-making, intuitive learning, trial and error, logic, analysis, communication, risk-taking, planning, resource management and computational thinking. Games encourage creativity and curiosity. Games give continuous assessment and do not punish players for making mistakes. Unlike an exam, failure is a work-in-progress. Simulation games are used as a training tool for pilots, surgeons, the armed forces and other professionals. Why not apply games-based learning to aspects of the national curriculum to add context? When playing a game like *Minecraft*, effectively digital LEGO®, a child learns that applying the heat of a furnace to silica sand produces glass, which they can put into their game world. Applied learning by doing is likely to be better understood than just being told facts. After selling his artificial intelligence company DeepMind to Google for some $400 million, British technology entrepreneur Demis Hassabis stated that, for him, playing games was a way of training the mind in multiple ways.

How does technology support pupils?

In a world where AI and robots will replace many jobs which involve repetition, children should be encouraged and rewarded for their creative flair. Creativity and computing are vital meta skills for the 21st century, and for an authentic modern curriculum, children need to learn the two Cs [creativity and computing] as well as the three Rs in school. Developing video games is the marriage of art and technology, requiring a combination of technical expertise and creative flair. The industry relies on a skilled workforce which adapts to furious rates of technological change. Unfortunately, the education system has not kept up with this change and is not meeting the needs of children who seek careers in the digital or creative industries. Of course, not every child will want to become a software engineer, but children need to know how code works. It would be a help to them in life to be in the driving seat of digital creativity, rather than the passenger seat of digital consumption.

Today, children have access to computers at school and in the home. They run their social lives through their mobile devices, immerse themselves in video games and get a top-up dose of ICT in the national curriculum. You would think that computing is one thing that no modern pupil is missing out on. Computing is no longer a marginal skill for experts and geeks – it's essential knowledge for competitive, innovative high-tech businesses. However, the narrowness by which some children learn about computing risks starving some of the UK's most successful industries of the talent they need to thrive. More resources urgently need to go into teaching the teachers. This is an important investment in the future.

In some schools, a convenient option was for children to simply use proprietary software in ICT lessons. However, focussing on office skills misses the point. Whilst Word, PowerPoint and Excel are useful in themselves, they give children no understanding of how to create their own software. It's like teaching children how to read, but not how to write. They can play a game but not make a game. At the Livingstone Academy Bournemouth, which opened in 2021 and is operated by Aspirations Academies Trust, the solution is not just to give every child a computer and basic ICT lessons and think 'job done'. Computers are a tool to enable digital creativity for the maker generation. Computer science is not just about coding. It's a discipline; a broad mix of computational thinking, problem-solving, decision making, intuitive learning, logic, analysis and creative thinking, to be used cross-curricula, to solve problems in multiple ways. In a world where computers define so much of how society works, from how we do business to how we enjoy ourselves, computer science is 'essential knowledge' for the 21st century. It could be argued that computer science is the new Latin, as it underpins the digital world in the same way Latin underpinned the analogue world.

Creativity gives the UK an edge as a nation, and it is essential that school is a place where young minds flourish. Imagination is key to the 'maker' generation. The arts should not be something which is simply 'nice to have', seen at best as a booster for other subjects, but not counting in the English Baccalaureate. The arts are often seen as a luxury, something which can be sacrificed in favour of more 'rigorous' subjects to which standardised tests and metrics can be applied. This is a grave misunderstanding of 'cultural value'. The creative industries are the fastest growing industrial sector in the UK economy (DCMS, 2023). Beyond the creative industries, the arts benefit all industries in terms of ideas creation, imagination, diverse thinking and self-determination. A good arts education improves cognitive abilities, confidence, motivation, problem-solving and communication skills. We must never underestimate the contribution that art, music, drama and design make in promoting diverse thinking, self-expression and self-determination. Because it is difficult to test or measure the intangible value of creativity, governments wrongly marginalise creative subjects in the curriculum on the grounds that students would be better served concentrating solely on STEM subjects to get a 'proper job'. This is an opportunity missed. Creative thinking is needed in all industries, from engineering to automotive to advertising. An authentic education for the digital world requires the government to evolve the curriculum, bringing the arts and sciences together to encourage innovation. By adding an 'A' for the arts, the mantra should be STEAM education, not STEM.

The challenges ahead

The Livingstone Academy adopts the STEAM model [science, technology, engineering, arts and maths] and encourages pupils to learn by doing, giving them real-world problems to solve, often in teams. All children are naturally curious and love solving problems. They enjoy doing things together. Human beings are all different, good at some things, bad at others. So, what is the point of standardised testing against the same metric in an examination? As the late Sir Ken Robinson pointed out (in a video by RSA, 2010), collaboration in schools is often seen as cheating, which is strange because that's how the workplace operates. The practice of teaching single subjects to the test risks redundancy by YouTube, online resources and peer-to-peer learning. Teaching needs to be in sync with 21st-century children. Education needs to reflect the world around us.

A curriculum based on knowledge recall is no longer relevant. The Livingstone Academy focuses on a skills-based approach to learning. We want our children to have skills as well as qualifications, and know-how as well as knowledge. They need to be work ready and world ready. We are not just training our pupils for jobs, but we do want to make sure they are well prepared for them. Many children in schools today will have jobs that do not yet exist, so there is no point in training them like robots, as [robots] won't be able to compete with the real thing. The World Economic Forum's ranking of the top three meta skills which children will need in the 21st century are problem-solving, critical thinking and creativity.

Just to be clear, it's not the case that children get to play games all day at the Livingstone Academy. Far from it. But games-based learning sets a great precedent as a model for problem-based cross-curricula learning and is important for the UK, which is more and more an ideas-based economy. The model has proved successful, especially for children who were traditionally taught, and often bored by, direct instruction. Instead of children being taught, for example, how to hit a nail with a hammer, at the Livingstone Academy the lesson might start, say, with a shelf. How would you design it? How would you build it? What do you need to build it? What about the materials themselves? Are they sustainable? What type of businesses make and sell shelves? And so on. They then form teams to further explore different aspects of the topic. The hammer and nails are simply tools and just part of the bigger picture project.

Busy secondary schools might argue that they have limited time to focus on cross-curricular learning, but we know how children benefit enormously from open-ended learning activities. The BBC's Computer Literacy Project in the 1980s not only helped to create a world-leading video game industry, but the technical skills learned by that generation went on to be applied creatively in fields as diverse as banking and medical imagery. We aim to steer children towards learning creative, digital skills which will help to equip them for the economies of their future – and have a lot of fun while they're doing it.

Whilst it is a state school with limited resources and the demands of Ofsted, the Livingstone Academy will strive to help its students navigate a world that is in constant change. We want our pupils to achieve good examination results through engaged learning at the same time as equipping them with know-how and skills for the 21st century digital world. If we encourage creativity and diverse thinking in children, give them the right digital-making skills, inspire an entrepreneurial mindset by letting them fail and learn from their mistakes, promote computational thinking and encourage them to collaborate, their future career ambition might change from being a job seeker to a job maker.

Another view

While our other interviewees advocate for the use of technology in the classroom setting, Pierre Laurent takes the opposite view explaining why – in his view – technology can breed anxiety, a lack of productivity, and even addiction. He advocates for a cautionary approach to ensure that we maintain a balance between making technology work efficiently for us without it potentially consuming our lives.

Pierre Laurent, School Administrator, Waldorf School of the Peninsula (WSP)

One of WSP's goals is to help students have a healthy relationship with technology. Tech should not be scary, mesmerising or evil. Technology brings tools that can help us become more productive and we have to understand these tools, when to use them, when not to use them and how they can change us.

Misused technology can lead students to lose focus, have unhealthy preoccupations and have difficulty creating and sustaining healthy relationships with peers and adults. When students are preoccupied by technology and overfed media and mediated experiences, their bandwidth to consider important questions to them and the world, and develop creativity, is greatly reduced.

Technology use by children, even when initially directed towards productive means, generally turns into unproductive usage, entertainment and media consumption. Those contributing to the media can lack individuality, and excessive consumption creates a uniform picture of what it is to be a teen to the detriment of personal growth and individualisation.

The effect of overuse of technology has been studied by psychologists, and several addiction centres around the world deal with the effects. Parents tend to consult these centres when they see extreme behaviours in their children, like suicide ideation, a drop in grades, or a lack of interest in school in teenagers. For many teenagers, the effects are not as extreme and parents do not feel they should take steps; yet smaller changes can be troublesome at the level of the individual or society. We see many changes in teenagers nowadays; the rise of anxiety is one example. Anxiety rose as tech rose, but correlation is not causation. The rise of technology also parallels and enables changes in parenting that could be the cause of anxiety. Thus, technology has had the effect of greatly amplifying the trend towards anxiety in young people. Technology brings convenience and can be the source of economic growth, individually and collectively, but it is not the magic wand to all problems, and careless usage at any age and in every situation may not always lead to the thoughtful outcomes parents wish for their child.

About 75% of our families have at least one parent who works in tech. It is precisely because [these parents] understand that technology does not teach you how to manage technology and that students need to develop human skills outside of technology to succeed and become experts of it, that [they] select our school for their children. The tech industry has been able to mostly ignore us because our voice is not large enough.

Around 2010, when most private schools advertised a 1:1 tablet/student ratio, we eschewed the trend. This was driven by our understanding of how children learn and what triggers learning. Modalities of learning depend on age. In our school, learning is calibrated with children's emotional, cognitive and physical development. Children learn best when they can physically engage with their environment, using their senses. A practical manipulation of blocks helps a student learn how to count in first grade, more than the manipulation of virtual blocks on the screen, because of the tactile, kinaesthetic and auditory nature of playing with blocks. Cutting and sharing a cake with the class is a better introduction to fractions than the virtual manipulation for the same concepts on a screen. Food sharing brings positive emotions, gustatory, olfactory and visual stimuli that a screen cannot provide. In high school, a puzzling science experiment designed, completed and observed by the students does more to draw interest in science than viewing the experiment on a screen. Emotions trigger learning and the best, sustainable emotions are the ones brought by the students' relationships with their parents, teachers and peers. Relationships mediated by technology are by nature incomplete and cannot achieve the same results.

In 2010, our teachers started using technology in their own lives. Computers, smartphones and tablets became ubiquitous in most teachers' homes. Since that time, we have not seen teaching mediated by technology in the classroom that could bring better outcomes than the human-centred experience. Of course, we use technology when it makes students more productive. In high school, they will write their essays on a computer and send them via email, but they will not do so in first grade as they form their writing, and we will not mediate student/teacher interactions with a computer.

Our method of education has always been known for fostering creativity. We understand creativity as not just 'making new things' or 'finding a new way to solve an old problem'. Creativity, at its core, is the ability to ask questions that have not yet been asked. From these questions, new trains of thoughts are born, new directions are taken. There is no app on the internet that truly develops creativity; this is because creativity is a unique human trait. It is at its best when the mind wanders freely, absent of preoccupations. Computers are no help and no match for that thinking process. Limiting technology usage is also a way to prevent the undue preoccupations that can pollute the creativity process.

As tech evolved and became more ubiquitous, with increased usage of social media, video and search at home, our role has been to keep the school mostly free from it, unless it serves a specific purpose, for instance learning proper usage of a search engine. We also developed classes for middle school and high school students to understand how tools can change them for better or worse, so that they can make their own technological choices, finding a healthy balance, only once they have the capacity to make that choice.

Reflections

Does technology understand education?

A number of interviewees in this chapter speak positively of working with technology companies, with those companies providing training and support. Matt Gibson at The Glasgow Academy shows a model where a school has taken advice from ed-tech specialists in order to create its own platform. Author and educator Robin MacPherson suggests that this sort of collaboration should go further and that technology companies should be seeking more guidance from schools on how children learn and be reminded of the possibility of reducing teacher workload (Hendrick and MacPherson, 2017).

What might these opportunities look like for schools and technology companies in the future? Would collaboration in these areas be a good use of time and resource for both schools and technology companies?

How should technology in schools be funded?

Neill Oldham, head teacher of Highfurlong School, describes how technology can be transformative in highly focused areas: for pupils with complex additional needs, technology can support them to fulfil their potential. In any school, technology that engages, inspires and assists pupils in areas they find challenging could be considered game changing; the difficulty might come in identifying how and at what point that technology should be made available. Should funding be similarly highly focussed within, for example, each state, MAT (multi-academy trust) or individual school?

Perhaps the future of technological innovation is not in schools, but *around* them. The Glasgow Academy's thinkfour is an attempt to fill the gaps in children's knowledge, and its authors are keen to ensure that not only is it free, but it is also free from collecting its users' data. Such an initiative, if it can be kept either free or cheap, is likely to appeal to schools struggling to fund training or the purchasing of new resources.

Where does technology fit in the school curriculum?

Technological policy and practice, for some schools, is developed by a small group of enthusiasts, rather than all the staff. In others, a significant amount of time is spent training staff in the necessary platforms and devices, sometimes by technology companies directly, as we heard from Highfurlong School, which also includes lessons on issues such as online safety and digital awareness within PSHE and relationships curricula. Phillip Hedger from the LEO Academy Trust talked of speaking to families and caregivers about topics such as screen time. At the Livingstone Academy, digital creativity, coding skills and tech entrepreneurism are placed front and centre, and used as a motivating factor to engage pupils with the rest of the national curriculum. Their argument is that by inspiring creativity, resilience and self-confidence through tech, it may be possible to benefit the learning elsewhere. And in doing so, you may also, incidentally, support social mobility and the development of powerful opportunities for young people who have been poorly served by more traditional educational models. It is a bold and fascinating vision which perhaps reflects the future direction of travel for other schools. Sir Ian's Next Gen review (Livingstone and Hope, 2011) was central in persuading the government at the time to put computer science on the national curriculum. Now he is a passionate advocate for 'using play to teach creative computing' (Livingstone and Saeed, 2016).

Some commentators have argued that Plato would have been a gamer. Unlike his sage and mentor, Socrates, Plato was quick to embrace 'writing things down' technology. He ignored the conservatism and scepticism of his great teacher, and decided to write down what Socrates had said, for posterity. The 'new' technology of our time, the explosion of the new online medium and its power to connect in ways that could not have been imagined even thirty years ago must, inevitably and surely, transform what learning is and what learning means for future generations. Whether it does so relatively swiftly, post-pandemic, or at a slower and more cautious pace, remains to be seen. It is likely to depend on factors such as investment in digital infrastructure and the urgency of need in the workplace. It will also, crucially, and as reflected in the comments made by several of our contributors, depend on our ability to respond to the pastoral implications of an increasingly technological world and our desire to hold on to the things that make us human in the real, 3D world.

Chapter 7

Wellbeing in schools

For many, schools in the past were places where you went to study and to get qualifications (or not). There are many famous accounts of life at independent schools, ranging from the poet Matthew Arnold at Rugby School to the politician Winston Churchill at Harrow, where any awareness of the interior life of a student by teachers was an unexpected bonus. Novels and memoirs set in miserable, dangerous schools with unwelcoming, harsh school masters are almost a sub-genre in themselves: in the work of writers such as Charles Dickens, with his depiction of Dotheboys Hall, or Evelyn Waugh, with his pitiless evocation of Llanabba.

But there are other stories, and they often come from perhaps unexpected sources. Arthur Christopher Benson was the personification of the Edwardian establishment. He was born in Wellington College (where a boarding house is still named after him) and spent much of his life teaching at Eton College, before becoming a lecturer in English at the University of Cambridge. He is perhaps best known today for writing the words to 'Land of Hope and Glory'. Benson wrote *The Schoolmaster* in 1902 and (at the time) it was a highly influential guide to young men who were considering becoming teachers. One might not expect this passage, describing the appeal of teaching, to come from such a figure as Benson:

'There is no profession which is so apt, if exercised faithfully and sympathetically and tenderly, to broaden the character and enlarge the spirit. A man who goes to be a schoolmaster with the expectation of having to discharge prescribed duties and afterwards to fill his leisure time as cheerfully as he may, suddenly wakes up to find himself in the grip of all kinds of problems; he finds himself found, like Gulliver, with all kinds of Lilliputian chains. The little people, who seem at first sight, to be all much alike in tastes and character, he realises are human beings with hearts and idiosyncrasies. He finds himself guiding and leading. The paternal, the protective instinct, which lies at the bottom of so many male hearts, wakes up; the man who began as the careless, self-regarding practitioner of a not very dignified trade, discovers that he is in the thick of a very real and vivid life, which stirs all sorts of interests and emotions and brings home to him some of the deep realities of life.' (2012 edition, p.6)

It does seem that, over time, teachers have become increasingly engaged with seeing into what educational researcher Graham Nuthall refers to in his 2007 book *The Hidden Lives of Learners* as the 'semi-private world of ongoing peer relationships'.

For example, in his 1975 book *The Craft of the Classroom*, Michael Marland shows an awareness of individual wellbeing and perhaps sensitivity in advising aspiring teachers to 'never refer to a pupil's family in front of other pupils' and, to never 'refer to physical or racial characteristics' (p. 19).

Jonathan Smith spent his whole career in independent schools and his autobiography, *The Learning Game*, was published in 2000. Smith describes teaching as a 'tricky business' because teachers have to strike a balance between caring and being disengaged from the complex lives of the children they teach.

In April 2006, in Benson's birthplace of Wellington College, its then headteacher, Anthony Seldon, announced that he planned to offer 'lessons in happiness' as the central part of the school's curriculum. In partnership with psychologist Nick Baylis and the University of Cambridge's Well-being Institute, the school developed a course predicated on the principles of positive psychology. There were two potentially paradigm shifting assertions embedded in this teaching programme. These were that a) schools had a direct and moral responsibility for ensuring the emotional wellbeing of their students and b) that emotional wellbeing or happiness is something that can be taught.

It is probably no accident that the focus on (and desire for) a more proactive approach to the teaching of wellbeing and strategies to help our children remain healthy and happy in schools also coincided with a growing unease and awareness about the levels of distress and mental health concerns in children. In the United Kingdom, a report published by the independent think tank Onward (Stanley et al., 2022) reports that between 2010 and 2018 the percentage of British children aged 16–24 reporting symptoms of depression or anxiety rose by 40%, from 18% to 25%. Furthermore, the rates of children with probable mental disorders has also increased since 2017, according to the Children's Commissioner (2023). The number of suicides by teens fell during the COVID-19 lockdown (McDonald, 2022), and then rose when in-person schooling started again (Morrison, 2022). In the UK, schools now have a responsibility to proactively teach pupils how to look after their wellbeing, as announced by the Department for Education and the (then) Secretary of State for Education, Damian Hinds, in 2019:

'All children in England will be taught how to look after their mental wellbeing... as the Government unveils new guidance for the introduction of compulsory health education... pupils of all ages will be taught the new subject – with a focus on promoting the positive link between physical and mental health... This comes alongside the introduction of compulsory relationships education for primary-age pupils and relationships and sex education (RSE) for secondary-age pupils, to ensure children have all the knowledge they need to grow up healthy, happy and safe.' (DfE, 2019b)

James Dahl, who is Master of Wellington College and was interviewed for this chapter, says that 'wellbeing will look, feel and mean different things to each individual child (and each individual member of staff)' which means it can be difficult to codify and explain what wellbeing learning involves. He is making the point that what works for one may not work for another. And, this is just one side of wellbeing. There is another focus for wellbeing which is perhaps even more levelling, as Jon Needham, the Director of Wellbeing and Safeguarding for the Oasis Multi-Academy Trust, reminds us. The schools in his trust serve areas of significant socio-economic deprivation. He talks of children with insecure family or caregiving networks, exposed to child exploitation, or with generations of disengaged and/or unemployed adults behind them. These children deal with threats to their physical, emotional and mental health which are challenging areas for schools to address. The risks of children being used as 'messengers' or 'carriers' across county lines by criminal gangs are very real, and make concerns about child wellbeing urgent and critical for schools operating in these areas. Needham suggests that pupil wellbeing in such circumstances is about staff in schools trying to find creative ways to break through deep, societal problems and entrenched community views – and that is not always easy. Oasis provide community support alongside education, ensuring a clear, widescale values-based approach which reinforces messages of hope and agency through and beyond the curriculum across all their schools. They also offer access to counsellors for staff as well as pupils but, as Needham points out, this all costs money and takes resources from other areas in schools.

The teachers we have spoken to have a clear, whole-hearted commitment to the holistic development of their pupils as well-rounded, well-grounded individuals with a strong sense of their own agency and efficacy. These are schools which have invested a great deal of time, thought and financial resources into providing educational wellbeing programmes and into ensuring that wellbeing is the yardstick by which all things in their schools are measured and assessed – from staff training to appraisal. But they are also candid about the difficulties and challenges that go along with this kind of focus.

Our contributors were candid about the risks of too much 'outsourcing' of wellbeing responsibility. Despite great care in the conveying of the message, Dominic A. A. Randolph of Riverdale Country School suggested that it is all too easy for children and teenagers to come away with the view that the school is solely responsible for their happiness and to develop a fragility or brittleness in the face of anything that might challenge that.

James Dahl of Wellington College suggests that following a wellbeing programme won't make you happy, it will simply give you the tools to manage whatever life throws at you. What do schools understand by the term wellbeing and how pivotal is it to the ethos of the school? What tools are available to schools in the provision of wellbeing? Can, and should, wellbeing be measured? If it is measured, how can one be sure these measurements provide accurate and useful data? We posed these questions to our interviewees.

Riverdale Country School

Fact file

Number of pupils: 1,270

Age range: 4–18

Co-educational/Single sex: Co-educational

Location: USA

State-funded/Independent: Independent

When was it established? 1907

Head/Contributor: Head: Kari Ostrem; Contributor: Dominic A. A. Randolph (Head of School 2007–2023)

Our pupils come from: 100 postal codes in the New York City area, including the Bronx, Manhattan, Brooklyn, Westchester County and New Jersey.

Our mission: Riverdale is a Pre-K through Grade 12 independent school in New York City committed to empowering lifelong learners by developing minds, building character, and creating community in order to change our world for the good.

Our vision and philosophy: Thriving and learning are inextricably intertwined. In the future we hope to prove that a school culture that fosters wellbeing leads to deeper and more effective learning.

How would you define wellbeing at your school, what characterises it and to what extent is it central to the identity of the school?

We started working on the connection between positive character strength development and both wellbeing and academic achievement in the early 2000s. This work led to a collaboration between the Knowledge is Power Program (KIPP) charter school network and Riverdale, involving working with leading social scientists such as Martin Seligman and Angela Duckworth to translate findings in the relatively new field of positive psychology into school practices. We have been promoting a culture of wellbeing in the school as a precondition for effective learning and living. Interestingly, some people view this focus as detracting from rigorous academic standards rather than being in support of academic excellence. Our mission and our key words – mind, character and community – support the idea that positive strengths, such as optimism, kindness and belonging, are instrumental in reaching for the best learning experiences we can possibly design. Therefore, learning and wellbeing are inextricably combined.

When we started this work with social scientists such as [psychology professors] Angela Duckworth and Ethan Kross in 2008–2009. Their work consisted of research projects that were individual experiments, seeking maximum impact. However, we don't believe that you change schools by serial experimentation. Therefore, we have focused more on fostering a culture of 'thriving + learning' suffused throughout the school. We have also moved to talk less about the goal of wellbeing, in preference for focusing on the means to wellbeing, such as increasing our experiential learning programme and offering more unstructured play experiences to our younger children that improve wellbeing.

Our mission, focused on developing minds, building character and creating belonging, is intimately linked to the concept of wellbeing and community thriving. We have recently rolled out the Thrive Project which focuses on the development of curiosity, purpose and belonging in concert with each other, to improve community wellbeing and thus improve learning in all domains. I think this broad view, that general thriving improves learning in all departments and programmes, helps ensure that every person in our community is thinking about their wellbeing.

Many schools only focus on wellbeing secondarily, if at all. We have been trying to move wellbeing to the foundation or core, without appearing to be losing our focus on high academic expectations. We try to disabuse people of the belief that this is an either/or proposition. We see wellbeing and learning as intimately entwined with each other.

What are the biggest challenges facing schools now, and in the future, when they try to protect and improve their pupils' wellbeing?

Recently in the United States, social emotional learning, character strengths and positive education have become linked to diversity work in schools and critical race theory, and therefore have become the target of the political right. This work is seen as linked to identity politics and seen as wrenching the role of developing their children from parents. This is very problematic. Also, the inability of people in our school community to understand that thriving is a precondition to good learning.

We have tried to ensure that we are promoting the wellbeing of *all* members of our community. Therefore, we have tons of programmes for faculty and staff: summer grants to pursue personal passions, daily yoga and fitness classes, coaching workshops. We believe it is essential to have this comprehensive view of community wellbeing. We also offer learning opportunities to parents.

Parents want both results and to see their children thriving. Interestingly, the two are completely connected, but rather than seeing the two as inextricably linked, many parents view them as two separate elements of their children's development. We have been trying to change this viewpoint, to have families understand that thriving is a precondition for effective learning.

Even though we believe that schools play an important and essential role in the development of wellbeing in children, we find ourselves more and more in challenging situations, where there are questions and confusion about the school's responsibilities.

Is there pathologisation of teenage behaviour?

Yes. There is a tension. We use the phrase 'warmly demanding' to describe teacher-student relationships. So, we believe that support and challenge come together to help students learn and develop. However, there are always tensions that need resolution. At times I believe we are, indeed, offering too much support, with the risk that that means we are developing people who always expect support and don't have the agency we would want them to develop.

But pathologisation is rife. It is a constant battle that needs to sort itself [out]. We have been lucky to hire counsellors who are pragmatic and who tend not to pathologise situations. However, this is a broader cultural problem, as is the suspicion of the mental health profession, which is not helpful either.

Wellington College

Fact file

Number of pupils: 1,100

Age range: 13–18

Co-educational/Single sex: Co-educational

Location: UK

State-funded/Independent: Independent

When was it established? 1859

Head/Contributor: James Dahl (Master)

Our pupils come from: 35–40 countries around the world. The majority of UK-based families live in London and the south east. Our international families are based in every corner of the globe.

Our values: Kindness, respect, courage, responsibility and integrity. These values were chosen by the Wellington community of students and staff following an in-depth consultation process over 15 years ago. They underpin everything from rewards and sanctions to our recruitment policies for both teachers and pupils.

Our academic vision: To inspire our students to become experts in subjects. We teach what makes the subject come alive and unlocks the special meaning created through each discipline. Depth is balanced with choice, with the IB Diploma and A-levels being taken by equal numbers in the sixth form.

Our pastoral vision: For every student to be known and treated as an individual. Proactive education through our Wellbeing programme and tutorials designed to equip our young people with the tools to cope with modern life is balanced by a team of professionals ready to react when issues and setbacks arise. In the future, the college intends to establish an educational research and professional development hub – The Bridge – to close the gap between classroom practice and research, and to support high-quality teaching across all settings. The Wellington family of international schools continues to grow, with schools due to open in India, Singapore, Malaysia and Indonesia to add to those in China and Thailand. A holistic Wellbeing Centre to bring together all aspects of proactive and reactive provision in physical and mental health is also in design.

How would you define wellbeing at your school, what characterises it and to what extent is it central to the identity of the school?

I would define wellbeing as thriving as a human being in all aspects of one's life. In the 2008 Foresight report, the authors defined it in this way:

Wellbeing is a 'dynamic state, in which the individual is able to develop their potential, work productively and creatively, build strong and positive relationships with others and contribute to their community. It is enhanced when an individual is able to fulfil their personal and social goals and achieve a sense of meaning and purpose in their society.' (2008, p. 10)

I think that still has a lot to commend it. But wellbeing will look, feel and mean different things to each individual child (and each individual member of staff). There will be common threads, of course, such as positive interpersonal relationships with others, a sense of meaning and purpose to our activities, healthy eating, sleep and exercise, etc. But plenty of differences, too. For example, we will contribute to our communities in different ways or we will nurture our different passions and interests in different ways.

In that sense, wellbeing is always going to be unfinished. Introducing fortnightly wellbeing lessons is one thing; weaving it into every strand of any organisation's operations is another. And although there are very few cynics about it now, it can feel that there is a tension between stress and wellbeing, especially in a school. Stress, for example in the run-up to examinations, is a natural part of life. Stress is not always bad for your mental health. A truly embedded wellbeing culture gives pupils and staff the tools to be able to cope with times of heightened stress and then to return to a more balanced state of holistic wellness after the moment has passed.

What are the biggest challenges facing schools now, and in the future, when they try to protect and improve their pupils' wellbeing?

One of the biggest challenges is that we have to change how wellbeing is perceived. It's not an 'either/or' scenario. Positive emotional health leads to better learning and academic advancement which, in itself, feeds into positive emotional health. We need to think of this as a double-helix structure, where the two are inextricably linked. It is an uncomfortable truth that many educational institutions with the highest rates of mental health issues are the highly academically intense and arguably competitive 'hot-house' environments, and this applies to schools and universities.

Other challenges which affect the wellbeing of our young people would, of course, include social media, and related to this, the comparison culture. Add to these the exacerbation of teenage mental health problems post-COVID-19 (including limited social interaction and an over-reliance on screens and the internet), and you can see that such things never seem to get any easier, for parents and for schools. We have to try to promote the idea that failure is acceptable, that being less than perfect is fine, and indeed that they contribute to our development as adults. These are big challenges, but I do think schools are making some progress, and at Wellington we are doing good work on de-stigmatising the conversation around mental health, and in particular around boys' and men's, mental health.

We try to avoid the gimmicky stuff: the yoga sessions and free coffee approach. We need to build genuinely supportive communities within our schools, which nurture a sense of strong moral purpose, foster autonomy, develop mastery, and where all staff (not just teachers) feel a genuine sense of belonging. The early wellbeing conversation in schools certainly focussed more around pupil wellbeing. At Wellington, we now devote as much time and thought to staff wellbeing, which is about managing workload and blending private- and work-life effectively. I also think that parents are increasingly aware of teenage mental health issues and are looking for schools that are trying to do something constructive about it. With Child and Adolescent Mental Health Services (CAMHS) waiting lists running at two years (Tidman, 2022), and the threshold for accessing professional support creeping ever higher, many parents are quite reasonably worried about their very reasonable expectations not being met by the wider system. This is why it is so incumbent upon schools to develop a wellbeing culture, with strategies which minimise the number of young people who even reach the threshold for professional help. This is a massive challenge in the state sector where budgets and funding for it are simply not there.

Is there pathologisation of teenage behaviour?

It's a question of balance, just as parenting is. It's about providing a framework which is fundamentally safe but which also encourages risk-taking and allows for failure. One can develop grit and resilience without ever being exposed to serious physical or psychological harm!

It is possible to look at it through a different lens: in the past, plenty of issues which should have been clinically diagnosed and treated were simply written off as 'part of growing up'. When my daughter says, 'This homework is bad for my mental health', she is clearly exaggerating. The process of learning new things, practising and mastering new skills and knowledge is a key way for young people to fulfil their potential and flourish as independent human beings. The key is in being able to differentiate between the natural emotional ebbs and flows, which are perfectly normal parts of the human condition, and emotions which are chronic, harmful and part of unhealthy illness. Those conditions where the usual day-to-day strategies won't provide the long-term relief, where therapeutic intervention is necessary. The work that we, and other schools, are trying to do will provide our young people and staff with a vocabulary that will, hopefully, help them make sense of perfectly normal, but complex feelings, and also know when they need help beyond themselves and when they need to seek professional advice. I can only see positives in this.

Oasis Community Learning – Multi-Academy Trust

Fact file

Number of pupils: 32,000

Age range: 4–18

Co-educational/Single sex: Co-educational

Location: UK

State-funded/Independent: State-funded

When was it established? 2004

Head/Contributor: Head: John Murphy (founder and CEO); Contributor: Jon Needham (National Director for Safeguarding and Mental Health)

Our pupils come from: All over. But 47% come from disadvantaged backgrounds and 31% speak English as an additional language.

Our values: We educate through a lens of character, competence and community. We have a commitment to inclusion, social integration and closing the disadvantage gap; we want to give advantage to the disadvantaged. Oasis staff aspire to create safe, stimulating learning environments, increase progress and attainment above national averages, and provide high-quality teaching which secures good and accelerated progress for all students.

Our academic vision: To offer exceptional education at the heart of the community.

Our pastoral vision: Grounded in our story, it is an expression of our character; a set of values that inform and provide the lens on everything we do:

- a passion to include
- a desire to treat people equally, respecting differences
- a commitment to healthy, open relationships
- a deep sense of hope that things can change and be transformed
- a sense of perseverance to keep going for the long haul.

It is these ethos values that we want to be known for and to live by. We are committed to a model of inclusion, equality, healthy relationships, hope and perseverance throughout all the aspects of the life and culture of every Oasis Hub and academy community.

We encourage every member of our family, be they staff or student, to align themselves to these ethos values. The values themselves are Christ-centred, but we make it clear that we will not impose on anyone the beliefs that underpin our ethos values. And we recognise and celebrate the richness that spiritual and cultural diversity brings to our community.

In the future: We will have five more schools joining our trust. And we hope government funding will enable a more holistic view of educating children.

How would you define wellbeing at your schools, what characterises it and to what extent is it central to the identity of the schools in your trust?

We are aiming for our children to be happy at school. We start with happiness because everything else comes from that. Of course, we measure that through outputs such as attendance and attainment; those are the things we can measure, and that inspections measure. But our starting point is wellbeing. If wellbeing is high, then the outputs will be good: attendance, attainment, engagement in learning; these are all outputs which reflect the fact that a child is happy in school.

So, for us, wellbeing means creating an environment that is suitable for every child to achieve their potential. We are confident that we have a consistent message around wellbeing which we set out clearly and support with staff training for all. It drives who we are. Fundamentally, we are a trauma-aware and a trauma-responsive organisation, rather than just a trauma-informed one. This means ensuring staff are alert to possible signals in our pupils. (For example, other schools might have staff standing at the door at 9.10am telling children off for being late and giving them detentions. We aim to do the opposite. We tell the kids who are arriving late, how pleased we are that they have managed to make it in. We say: 'Yes, you're a little bit late, but at least you are here.' We start our phone calls chasing up attendance with this message: 'We missed you at school today. You make a difference to our class. It wasn't the same because you weren't here.') The trick is to take steps that emphasise the positive, rather than the punitive, so that school feels like somewhere our children want to be.

We don't follow the national curriculum, we follow our own Oasis curriculum and it is built around what we call 'the nine habits'. All our assemblies reflect the habits and we have a habit of the month. We have newsletters which the kids all contribute to. It is part of our everyday language. I will often ask pupils as they come into school: 'Which habit are you most identifying with today?' It is absolutely built into our ethos, our language, our approach across the trust. And the habits are all things that you would want to be yourself: joyful, compassionate, forgiving, honest, patient, humble, hopeful, self-controlled and considerate. They are habits which promote individual wellbeing, self-development and self-growth, but they are also what you need if you are going to live well in a community.

Alongside this, we have 100 things that we want our pupils to experience as part of their time in one of our primary or secondary schools. These include things like trips to the theatre, a trip to the seaside, kicking through autumn leaves somewhere lovely… It's a key part of who we are.

What are the biggest challenges facing schools now, and in the future, when they try to protect and improve their pupils' wellbeing?

All of our schools are in high areas of deprivation, and whilst it's not inevitable that if you live in a very deprived area you will have lower levels of parental engagement with schools, we nonetheless do find it harder to engage families in areas of social deprivation. We have schools where the parents are out of work, the grandparents are out of work, the great-grandparents are out of work. It's baked in. There is very little incentive for education in these family environments. Their attitude is: Why should I force my kid to go to school? School doesn't lead anywhere. So, this is the social hurdle we need to get over as well. And it is never straightforward to do that.

At Oasis, we make it clear that we cannot guarantee our children will always be safe, because we are only responsible for five or six hours of that child's life every day. We can make them *safer*. And that's what we commit, entirely, to do. A lot of the stuff we do around e-safety will, absolutely, make a child safer. But we can't guarantee to keep a child safe 24 hours a day, because that would be to set unrealistic expectations. Again, it comes down to parents. We know, for example, that a parent should be monitoring their child's use of the internet. We can teach children how to be safer on the internet, we can teach them to look out for the risks and dangers online. We can do that in school. But ultimately, it is the parents' responsibility to ensure that their child is not logging onto a site they should not be accessing at 2am. There are a number of big wellbeing worries for us at the moment. Knife crime and street violence are huge concerns. And these are directly linked to child criminal exploitation, county lines exploitation. If you've got a 15-year-old kid who can make £500 a week selling drugs, and they've got two parents (if they're lucky) with no income or, more likely, a single parent with no job and no income, how can you persuade that 15-year-old not to sell drugs? They know that by doing so they can become the breadwinner for their family. It is such a difficult issue for schools to address and providing a counter to that kind of narrative is a big preoccupation for us. Alongside that, of course, there is the usual concern about increases in poor mental health.

And the truth is, there is work to be done in terms of getting buy-in from all our parents. I was talking to somebody yesterday who recounted the fact that a parent had come up to a new headteacher in one of our schools and said: 'This school is crap'. The headteacher replied: 'OK, so what are *you* going to do to help me make it a better school?' and that parent was completely flummoxed! The point is, strong wellbeing outcomes depend on having a strong parent-school partnership. Getting children into school depends on parents taking responsibility. Most of our attendance issues at primary level are nothing to do with children and all to do with parents not getting themselves sufficiently organised to get their child into school on time. The skill is getting the parents on board with that message. And we work hard to do that. We talk about our ethos with parents: we have parents' evenings, reading logs, learning logs… we have all those things, but fundamentally, if the parent doesn't buy into it, schools are left just trying to cope with it.

Another big challenge for us, in terms of maintaining pupil wellbeing, is the wider role we feel our schools have to play in the community, given the levels of economic deprivation around our schools. Our ethos is for our schools to be at the centre of our local community and to play a key part in that community. That's an important aspect of improving pupil wellbeing too.

We have community hubs offering either food pantries, food banks or adult education sessions, attached to almost all of our 52 schools. Right now, for example, a number of our schools are running something called 'warm front rooms' in response to the heating crisis, where families can come and be warm and have some soup and a hot drink. This matters for some of our school communities of course. Providing somewhere safe and warm for children to do their homework, or helping to feed a family so that our parents can parent more successfully, has obvious wellbeing benefits.

But there's a challenge here to do with funding. Some think: Why should a random person with no direct connection to our schools have access to a food pantry or a safe and warm environment offered by our school? What's that got to do with our pupils' wellbeing or education? We feel very strongly that we can't exclude the old man who lives next door to one of our schools and is cold and hungry from our services just because he is not directly connected with that school. What kind of message would that give the children? It is counter to our values and to what we want our children to learn.

So, this inevitably puts pressure on our staff and it is hard for our headteachers who are having to manage wider community issues which are distressing and potentially distracting, given that they also need to focus on school attainment, which, again, is what they are measured against. So, these are very real pressures which our schools are having to absorb at the moment.

Funding to promote pupil wellbeing is also a serious challenge for all our schools. Oasis has just commissioned a report by Anne Longfield (the Children's

Commissioner for England in 2022) on the needs of extremely vulnerable children. The report identified that kids with complex social and emotional and learning and community needs require an A-Team around the family to support them. It's not just about the pupil's needs; if the child is to succeed, it is about providing proper support to the wider family and community around that child.

There's no big surprise in that. We have known about it for a while. And schools are well placed to deliver this support and to help with the coordinating of different agencies. But the Treasury view on funding for children at school is basically vertical. The money comes from the government direct to schools to deliver education in a straight vertical line, direct to the child. Longfield's report suggests that funding, at a school level, needs to be more horizontal. We need to fund counselling services, food banks and other kinds of community support, which will enable that child to be ready to learn and to achieve their A levels or GCSEs.

And the truth is, this is a problem which is getting worse. We categorise pupil mental health needs into four levels against five different criteria, including whether they are whole-school issues, intermediate issues or high-need/high-risk issues. Currently, our high-need/high-risk demands are huge. We are trying to put the right support team in place to deal with this level of need, because we know we can no longer rely on Child and Adolescent Mental Health Services (CAMHS), but that costs a lot. I have a current bid in, to the trust, to fund this team to the tune of £1 million to support all our schools across the country. But I am well aware that to do that, we will have to lose something else. We're not going to compromise on the academic provision because that's the core function of a school. So, we've got to take from somewhere else. Where is it going to come from? From IT? From our HR support? Are we going to take it from the 'properties and estates' budget somehow? These are very tough questions.

Also, of course, there's the issue of staff responsibility. All our staff recognise that safeguarding is everybody's responsibility. That they all need to be alert, be responsive and refer issues to the designated safeguarding lead (DSL) and the deputy DSL if and when necessary. Which of course is great. But, the view can be: 'Great, I've done my job, because I've let the DSL know…'. And that is true both of safeguarding and wider issues to do with pupil health and wellbeing. Everybody recognises how important it is for kids to be happy in class, but it can be all too easy for teachers to focus on the academic learning in their lessons because they've got to deliver on targets against which they are being measured. And that is all the more the case when the pressure is on, when the magnifying glass is on an individual's performance, or when there is pressure from Ofsted. Staff can quickly revert to: 'I've got to get my attainment up. I've got to sort the SATs. I've got to ensure the right GCSE scores… So, that's what I'll do and I'll pass the other stuff on to the pastoral team…'. That is an ongoing challenge because Ofsted explicitly measures academic attainment, not mental health or wellbeing outcomes.

Is there pathologisation of teenage behaviour?

One of the things that we are spending a lot of time on, in our schools, is identifying what is a 'normal' mood, a normal feature of adolescence, and what is a real mental health issue. Because so many people now are saying to us: 'I've got anxiety, I've got depression...'. And the truth is, they haven't. What they've got is a perfectly normal worry about exams or about their future. And that's perfectly normal. Anxiety and depression are diagnosable conditions. We are seeking to educate staff and pupils around the differences here.

So, we employ external counselling agencies on contracted hours in our schools. And part of my job is to ensure we have key performance indicators in place, to ensure that the counsellors are worth the money we are investing in them.

Another view

Here, Dr James Davies provides a different, although arguably no less compassionate, perspective on wellbeing provision in schools. He presents the argument that diagnosis of disorders may in fact exaggerate behaviour that would otherwise be viewed as part of the complex journey through adolescence. He concedes that socio-economic factors play a huge part in the lives of many young people in the ways identified by the contributors. He does note that it is perhaps increasingly challenging for teachers to be able to recognise differences between genuine long-term issues and temporary difficulties experienced by young people.

Dr James Davies, Associate Professor of Medical Anthropology and Psychology at the University of Roehampton

In the last two decades, poor mental health in children has increased rapidly, along with the pressure on schools and teachers to address it in medicalised ways. The result has been an explosion of initiatives, specifically designed to help teachers better identify and help vulnerable children early on, and to safeguard against more serious interventions being needed at a later stage.

One such recent and relevant study showed that, due to these programmes, teachers are now more likely to interpret children's behaviours and feelings as indicating mental health problems than they were only ten years ago. This has created heightened anxiety in teachers about what childhood distress could mean (Timimi and Timimi, 2022). Fear about failing to identify problems early enough meant that much behaviour previously considered ordinary and understandable (given the difficult conditions children struggle with) was now more often thought of as indicating mental health problems, needing expert help. Ordinary experiences like peer break-ups, being younger in the classroom or failing to concentrate were increasingly falling under the medicalised rubric of disorder (Newlan, 2018). Furthermore, teachers were finding it ever more difficult to differentiate between children who had 'mental health conditions' or those who were naughty or even misused their diagnoses to deny responsibility for their behaviour. Teachers appeared increasingly confused about what behaviour should be dealt with in a disciplinary way, and what problems required more sympathy or should be referred on.

These findings indicate that mental health school programmes are subtly socialising teachers to distrust their own social and pedagogical instincts and rather to defer to highly medicalised ways of framing and responding to distress. Rather than regarding distress as a protest against harmful social and relational conditions, teachers are being taught to reframe it, as pointing to internal dysfunctions requiring 'early intervention'.

Moving forward, an increasing number of academics, psychologists and researchers are now beginning to argue for a new approach; one that does not locate the solution to our childhood mental health crisis in more access to mental health services, more mental health care in our schools, or even more teachers trained in emotional literacy. Rather, it is calling for a profound rethinking of the nature of childhood suffering itself, and what it is trying to highlight and ask us to change. It calls on teachers, parents and policy makers to understand emotional distress in more sociological ways, rather than to continue reducing it to dysfunctions that allegedly reside within children's selves. It calls on us to acknowledge that suffering also reflects family and socio-political dynamics we would do well to better acknowledge and address. As the renowned clinical psychologist, Professor Anne Cooke, stated: 'The mental illness narrative encourages us to see mental health problems as nothing to do with life and circumstances, so no wonder we don't look at structural or social causes; and of course this perspective is a great fit with the current neoliberal approach – where individuals have to reform themselves, to fit with existing social structures' (cited in Davies, 2021, page 89). The trouble with programmes that ignore the perils of such adaptations is that they essentially neuter reflection on why distress proliferates in our schools, certainly when compared to schools in most other developed nations (Govorova et al., 2020; OECD, 2009). Instead, we resort to medicalisation, which shores up existing social conditions with interventions and meanings that individualise distress.

In the end, it is the ability of mental health interventions to obscure the social roots of distress where they perhaps cast their longest shadow. An essential part of any remedy is therefore learning to understand and critically assess the wider forces holding our children back. We must accept that, for many children, the truest and most effective therapy won't be found in a pill, a consultancy room, or even in a classroom intervention, but in loving and meaningful human relationships that endeavour to mitigate the harsher social forces and impacts that children neither manage nor understand.

Reflections

Can you teach wellbeing?

All the heads that we have spoken to, to inform this chapter, are strong proponents of wellbeing on the curriculum. In addition, Jon Needham of Oasis Community Learning mentioned specific teaching opportunities for wellbeing, for example through their e-safety lessons as well as 'nine habits' teaching in assemblies and newsletters. Dominic A. A. Randolph of Riverdale Country School also talked about learning opportunities they offer to parents. However, the general theme from interviewees was that teaching wellbeing was not enough on its own.

For Oasis Community Learning, wellbeing perhaps starts with what we might consider fundamentals: community hubs that can offer safe, warm spaces and food banks, for example. Jon Needham also explained that they have 100 things that they want their pupils to experience before they leave the school; experiences that will enrich their lives. Perhaps along a similar vein, Riverdale Country School have an 'experiential learning programme' which Dominic A. A. Randolph sees as an important means to wellbeing. This programme includes 'service-learning, global studies, outdoor/adventure education, community engagement, and interdisciplinary programs' (Riverdale, no date). Their new 'Thrive Project' focussing on developing curiosity, purpose and belonging is also considered another means to wellbeing.

Part of this experiential learning is no doubt through teacher-pupil interactions and relationships, as mentioned by Dominic A. A. Randolph and in the sense of belonging and community that each school highlighted. More than this, there was also a strong sense that staff wellbeing was as important as pupil wellbeing in order to enable what James Dahl called 'genuinely supportive communities within our schools'. Oasis extend this even further to parent and family wellbeing and even the wellbeing of the wider community to provide a broad vision of wellbeing and what it might look like. To what extent might there already be experiential learning programmes in schools fulfilling the roles described above? Is it possible or desirable for schools to promote the wellbeing of parents and caregivers or even those in the wider community? If so, what could that look like?

Conclusion

It has been a great privilege for us to be able to visit schools, talk to their leaders, and find out why parents have decided to choose a particular school as research for this book. Whilst necessarily only fractional in number, we have sought out schools, in the UK and beyond, which are interesting, distinctive and highly committed to their specific educational approach. And whether the schools are old or new, in the UK or elsewhere, independent or state, ancient or very new, they are all characterised by having leaders who are able to express clearly, with conviction and great enthusiasm, what they are and why that is the case. We think that such schools are a fundamental part of a rich 'ecosystem' of models, including independent, state, selective, comprehensive, faith, secular, single-sex, co-educational, traditional, creative and so on.

The aim of this book is to promote debate and encourage reflection for you as readers in your own schools and contexts. What concluding questions, then, can we pose to you?

It is axiomatic to say that schools are complex places. They are made up of many 'moving parts': pupils and teachers (of course) and also support staff, governors, parents and, beyond that, all the organisations and companies that keep a school functioning: social services, local education authorities or districts, consultants, assessment bodies, inspection teams, caterers, security companies, buses, taxis... the list goes on. The schools we spoke to are largely predicated on one organising idea. They promote and value a particular aspect or approach above everything else. Did that make discussions and disputes about pedagogy, values, priorities, resourcing and development clearer? Our interviewees suggested that a commonality of understanding – of the school and beyond – can be a very useful unifying idea in the midst of other considerations.

The leaders we spoke to felt able to sustain progress (even with less time than they might wish for), because of the distinctive approaches they take. Some schools change voluntarily, but most have had change thrust upon them, and it would be interesting to revisit our schools in five years' time to see how they have adapted to new challenges. Would COVID-19 still be discussed? How much might the taught curriculum or school policies have changed? What sort of language will be used, and behaviours promoted? What sort of technology will be used in the classroom and beyond? Would their distinctive values help in new changes and decisions? Greek philosopher Heraclitus said: 'Change is the only constant in life'. The school leaders we spoke to, and their staff, pupils and parents, value the permanence of their school's values. They suggest that there is something innately appealing to say to yourself, and to parents: 'This is what we do, this is what we cherish, this is what we put at the core of who we are'. It does not discount an ongoing evolution but it acts as a marker or, to change metaphors, a compass that helps guide the school into the future.

We have also learned from talking to leaders that for a school to have its values deeply embedded in its DNA, they have to be wider and deeper than any one person's individual vision. How can this be done? Schools, like other organisations that you inhabit or interact with during formative periods of life, tend to have more community habits and traditions than others. As we have seen from the schools we interviewed, each will have a language, a set of conventions that help define who and what they are. And these conventions can outlast the students, the teachers, the heads, the chairs and so on. The school leaders we talked to were aware of what they have inherited, what they are custodians of, and the question for each of them, as well as for us, is how they can preserve the distinctive ethos of a school, without confining the school to a life imprisoned by its past. How can a culture be changed or maintained? Is it possible to cultivate a sense of hope and optimism and if so, how? The leaders we talked to often valued debate, were open to self-reflection, and took nothing for granted. What other sorts of characteristics might be needed in school leaders?

Writing in 1910, in the midst of the economic, industrial and political turbulence at the start of his own new century, E. M. Forster exhorted us all to: 'only connect the prose and the passion and both will be exalted... human love will be seen at its height. Live in fragments no longer' (Forster, 1910, p. 195). Only connect! That is what the schools we have spoken to, and schools in general, can enable. Can a school have a strong, convincing and authentic identity? How is that communicated clearly to its stakeholders and subscribed to by its constituents? How can a school connect its pupils to the historic story and shared past of the school, to the world as they find it now and, most exciting of all, to the unknowable, unimaginable futures they are going to be heading out to find and to shape? Each of the schools had different answers to these questions and no doubt you as a reader will too.

This book was imagined just before the pandemic and then COVID-19 came and turned everything (including our timescales) upside down! Nonetheless, we have had conversations and experiences in schools that are all the richer because of the shared, seismic, global disruption we have all been through and emerged from. We are hugely grateful to those inspiring and exciting school leaders featured in this book, who were prepared, either during the pandemic or after it, to show us their schools, to explain their mission and vision, to inspire us with their belief and enthusiasm for their institutions and – we hope – to promote questions and reflection in your mind about what your school can be.

References

Accord (2012), 'Nearly three quarters of the British public disagrees with religious selection in admissions at state funded schools', https://accordcoalition.org.uk/2012/11/12/nea rly-three-quarters-of-the-british-public-disagrees-with-religious-selection-in-admissi ons-at-state-funded-schools/

AQR International (2021), 'Soft skills development and gender an analysis of mental toughness at UK independent schools', https://gsa.uk.com/wp-content/uploads-gsa/2021/06/AQR-analysis-of-mental-toughness-in-girls-schools.pdf

Archard, N. (2012), 'Adolescent girls and leadership: The impact of confidence, competition, and failure', *International Journal of Adolescence and Youth*, 17, (4), 189–203.

Ashman, G. (2018), 'We don't need no Sir Ken Robinson', Filling the Pail, https://gregash man.wordpress.com/2018/03/24/we-dont-need-no-sir-ken-robinson

Aubrey-Smith, F. (2021), 'Forget edtech – we need to talk about "pedtech"', *Headteacher Update*, 7 June 2021, www.headteacher-update.com/best-practice-article/forget-edt ech-we-need-to-talk-about-pedtech-technology-learning-schools-classrooms-teach ers-1/237834

Baker, J. and Gladstone, N. (2022), 'Girls now out-performing boys in nearly every HSC subject', *The Sydney Morning Herald*, 11 December 2022, https://www.smh.com.au/natio nal/nsw/girls-now-out-performing-boys-in-nearly-every-hsc-subject-20221209-p5c 56d.html

Barenberg, J., Roeder, U.-R. and Dutke, S. (2018), 'Students' temporal distributing of learning activities in psychology courses: Factors of influence and effects on the metacognitive learning outcome', *Psychology Learning & Teaching*, 17, (3), 257–271.

BBC News (2021), 'Digital divide "locking children out of education"', https://www.bbc. co.uk/news/uk-england-55816686

Benson, A. C. (2012), *The Schoolmaster; A Commentary Upon the Aims and Methods of an Assistant-Master in a Public School*. Woodbridge: Peridot Press.

Birbalsingh, K. (2021), [*X, formerly Twitter*] 26 September 2021, @Miss_Snuffy, https://twit ter.com/Miss_Snuffy/status/1442084998992089090

Blaff, A. (2023), '2 + 2 = white supremacy: How woke ideologues corrupted Canada's math curriculum', *National Review*, www.nationalreview.com/news/22white-suprem acy-how-woke-ideologues-corrupted-canadas-math-curriculum

Blumberg, M. (2011), 'First Rate Intelligence', *Insider*, https://www.businessinsider.com/ first-rate-intelligence-2011-4?r=US&IR=T

Brassington, L. (2022), 'Gypsies, Roma and Travellers: The ethnic minorities most excluded from UK education' https://www.hepi.ac.uk/wp-content/uploads/2022/07/Gyps ies-Roma-and-Travellers.pdf

Brighouse, T. and Waters, M. (2022), *About Our Schools: Improving on Previous Best*. Carmarthen: Crown House Publishing.

Brooks, D. (2017), 'How to leave a mark on people', *New York Times*, www.nytimes.com/2017/04/18/opinion/how-to-leave-a-mark-on-people.html

Busette, C. (2018), 'A new deal for poor African-American and Native-American boys', *Brookings*, www.brookings.edu/blog/fixgov/2018/03/14/a-new-deal-for-poor-african-american-and-native-american-boys

Caplan, B. (2023), 'The joyless polity', Stumbling and Mumbling, https://stumblingandmumbling.typepad.com/stumbling_and_mumbling

Carey, B. (2014), *How We Learn: The Surprising Truth About When, Where, and Why It Happens.* New York: Random House.

Centers for Disease Control and Prevention (CDC) (2023), 'CDC releases the Youth Risk Behavior Survey Data Summary & Trends Report: 2011–2021', www.cdc.gov/nchhstp/dear_colleague/2023/DSRT-DCL.html

Chan Zuckerberg Initiative (2022), 'Super-powering student motivation and engagement', https://chanzuckerberg.com/newsroom/super-powering-student-motivation-and-engagement

Children's Commissioner (2023), 'Children's mental health services 2021–2022', www.childrenscommissioner.gov.uk/resource/29751/

Christodoulou, D. (2014), *Seven Myths about Education.* Abingdon: Routledge.

Christodoulou, D. (2015), 'Debating education review', Daisy Christodoulou, https://daisychristodoulou.com/2015/11/debating-education-review

Christodoulou, D. (2017), *Making Good Progress? The future of Assessment for Learning.* Oxford: Oxford University Press.

Christodoulou, D. (2023), 'Can ChatGPT give feedback?', https://blog.nomoremarking.com/can-chatgpt-give-feedback-12d3b736eba9

Christov-Moore, L., Simpson, E. A., Coudé, G., Grigaityte, K., Iacoboni, M. and Francesco Ferrari, P. (2014), 'Empathy: Gender effects in brain and behaviour', *Neuroscience & Biobehavioral Reviews*, 46, Pt 4(Pt 4), 604–27.

Clery E., Curtice, J. and Harding R. (2016), British Social Attitudes: The 34th Report, London: NatCen Social Research, www.bsa.natcen.ac.uk https://bsa.natcen.ac.uk/media/39196/bsa34_full-report_fin.pdf

Coe, R. (2013), 'Improving education: A triumph of hope over experience', CEM, Durham University, http://eachandeverydog.net/wp-content/uploads/2015/05/ImprovingEducation2013.pdf

Craft, A. (2000), *Creativity Across the Primary Curriculum: Framing and Developing Practice.* London, New York: Routledge.

Creativity Exchange. (no date), 'Welcome to The Creativity Exchange', https://www.creativityexchange.org.uk/

Cribb, V. L. and Haase, A. M. (2016), 'Girls feeling good at school: School gender environment, internalization and awareness of socio-cultural attitudes associations with self-esteem in adolescent girls', *Journal of Adolescence*, 46, 107–114.

Davies, J. (2021), *Sedated: How Modern Capitalism Created our Mental Health Crisis.* London: Atlantic Books.

De Beauvoir, S. (1949), *The Second Sex (Le Deuxième Sexe).* France: Librarie Gallimard.

Department for Culture, Media and Sport (DCMS) (2023), 'Ambitious plans to grow the economy and boost creative industries', https://www.gov.uk/government/news/ambitious-plans-to-grow-the-economy-and-boost-creative-industries

Department for Education (DfE) (2019a), 'Schools, pupils and their characteristics: January 2019', https://www.gov.uk/government/statistics/schools-pupils-and-their-characteristics-january-2019

Department for Education (DfE) (2019b), 'All pupils will be taught about mental and physical wellbeing', https://www.gov.uk/government/news/all-pupils-will-be-taught-about-mental-and-physical-wellbeing

Department for Education (DfE) (2021), 'Free School Meals, Gender and Ethnic Group' from 'Widening participation in higher education', https://explore-education-statistics. service.gov.uk/data-tables/permalink/77f3aabf-1e21-4c2f-bb58-b5671c695307

Department for Education (DfE) (2023), 'Generative artificial intelligence in education: Departmental statement', https://assets.publishing.service.gov.uk/governm ent/uploads/system/uploads/attachment_data/file/1146540/Generative_artificial_intelli gence_in_education_.pdf

Didau, D. (2014), 'The dark art of creativity', David Didau, https://learningspy.co.uk/myths/ dark-art-creativity

Duffy, J. (2022), 'OCR adds diverse voices to poetry for GCSE English Literature – with greater diversity in more qualifications in 2023', OCR, https://www.ocr.org.uk/news/ ocr-adds-diverse-voices-to-poetry-for-gcse-english-literature

Durham Commission (2019), 'Durham Commission on Creativity and Education', Durham University and Arts Council England, www.artscouncil.org.uk/sites/default/files/downl oad-file/Durham_Commission_on_Creativity_04112019_0.pdf

Education Endowment Foundation (no date), 'Collaborative learning approaches', https:// educationendowmentfoundation.org.uk/education-evidence/teaching-learning-toolkit/ collaborative-learning-approaches

Eliot, L. (2019), 'Neurosexism: the myth that men and women have different brains', *Nature*, https://www.nature.com/articles/d41586-019-00677-x

Emerich France, P. (2018), 'Why I left Silicon Valley, edtech, and "personalized" learning', Make Teaching Sustainable, https://maketeachingsustainable.org/blog/2018/01/15/ why-i-left-silicon-valley-edtech-and-personalized-learning

Ericsson, A. and Poole, R. (2016), *Peak: Secrets from the New Science of Expertise.* Boston: Houghton Mifflin Harcourt.

Fine, C. (2010), *Delusions of Gender: The Real Science Behind Sex Differences.* London: Icon Books.

Fisher, J., Forgasz, H. and Lang, C. (2015), 'Girls gain confidence with IT when boys aren't around', https://www.monash.edu/news/opinions/girls-gain-confide nce-with-it-when-boys-arent-around

Fitzgerald, F. S. (1936), 'The Crack-Up', *Esquire* republished in 2017 https://www.esquire. com/lifestyle/a4310/the-crack-up/#ixzz1Fvs5lu8w

Fitzsimmons, T.W., Yates, M. S., and Callan, V. (2018), 'Hands Up for Gender Equality: A Major Study into Confidence and Career Intentions of Adolescent Girls and Boys', Brisbane, Qld: AIBE Centre for Gender Equality in the Workplace – The University of Queensland.

Fitzsimmons, T. W., Yates, M. S., and Callan, V. J. (2021), 'Lean in? The role of single sex schools in the gendering of confidence in high school adolescents', *Australian Journal of Career Development*, 30(2), 139–149.

Foresight Mental Capital and Wellbeing Project (2008), 'Final project report: Executive summary', The Government Office for Science, https://assets.publishing.service.gov. uk/government/uploads/system/uploads/attachment_data/file/292453/mental-capital-wellbeing-summary.pdf

Forster, E. M. (1910), *Howards End.* New York: Alfred A. Knopf. Reprinted 1991, Germany: David Campbell Publishers.

Fortin, M., Oreopoulos, P. & Phipps, S. (2013), 'Leaving Boys Behind: Gender Disparities in High Academic Achievement', *NBER Working Paper Series*, Vol 19331.

Franklin, P. (2018), 'The ideological battle over classroom seating arrangements', UnHerd, https://unherd.com/2018/02/ideological-battle-classroom-seating-arrangements

Geelong Grammar School (no date), 'What is positive education?', www.ggs.vic.edu.au/learn ing/wellbeing/what-is-positive-education

Gentrup, S. and Rjosk, C. (2018), 'Pygmalion and the gender gap: Do teacher expectations contribute to differences in achievement between boys and girls at the beginning of schooling?' *Educational Research and Evaluation*, 3–5, (24), 295–323.

Gladwell, M. (2008), *Outliers: The Story of Success*. New York: Little, Brown and Company.

Gladwell, M. (2013), 'Complexity and the ten-thousand-hour rule', *New Yorker*, www.newyor ker.com/sports/sporting-scene/complexity-and-the-ten-thousand-hour-rule

GOV.UK. (no date), *Music and Dance Scheme: funding for students*, https://www.gov.uk/music-dance-scheme

Gove, M. (2012), 'Speech: Secretary of State for Education Michael Gove gives speech to IAA', www.gov.uk/government/speeches/secretary-of-state-for-education-mich ael-gove-gives-speech-to-iaa

Govorova, E., Benítez, I. and Muñiz, J. (2020), 'How schools affect student well-being: A cross-cultural approach in 35 OECD countries', *Frontiers in Psychology*, 11, 431.

Gray, J. (1992), *Men Are From Mars, Women Are From Venus*. New York: HarperCollins.

Grey, M. G. and Shirreff, E. (1850), *Thoughts on Self-Culture, Addressed to Women* (vol 1). London: Edward Moxon.

Haidt, J. (2023), 'Why the mental health of liberal girls sank first and fastest', After Babel, https://jonathanhaidt.substack.com/p/mental-health-liberal-girls

Haidt, J. and Lukianoff, G. (2019), *The Coddling of the American Mind*. Harlow, UK: Penguin Books.

Hausmann, R. (2015), 'The education myth', Project Syndicate, www.project-syndicate.org/commentary/education-economic-growth-by-ricardo-hausmann-2015-05

Hendrick, C. and MacPherson, R. (2017), *What Does This Look Like in the Classroom?* Woodbridge: John Catt.

Hinds, D. (2019), 'Press release: All pupils will be taught about mental and physical wellbeing', Department for Education, www.gov.uk/government/news/all-pupils-will-be-tau ght-about-mental-and-physical-wellbeing

Hirsch, E. D. (1988), *Cultural Literacy: What Every American Needs to Know*. New York: Vintage Books.

Hirsch, E. D. (1999), *The Schools We Need*. New York: Anchor Books.

Hofer, S. (2015), 'Studying Gender Bias in Physics Grading: The role of teaching experience and country', *International Journal of Science Education*, 37, (17), 2879–2905.

Hoffnung, M. (2011), 'Career and Family Outcomes for Women Graduates of Single-Sex Versus Coed Colleges', *Sex Roles*, 65, 680–692.

Hoxby, C. (2006), 'The Power of Peers', Education Next, https://www.educationnext.org/the-power-of-peers/

Hughes, C. (2023), 'The necessity to broaden education and how we can do it', Ecolint, https://drive.google.com/file/d/1jlDgM8wTi0kYfwSh-_nXJ7bJDTI2HnBW/view?pli=1

Humanists UK (2020a), '40% of independent faith schools fail to meet Ofsted standards with Steiner schools also failing badly', https://humanists.uk/2020/01/22/40-of-independ ent-faith-schools-fail-to-meet-ofsted-standards-with-steiner-schools-failing-badly/

Humanists UK (2020b), 'Faith-based school admissions disadvantage non-religious and minorities, Humanists UK tells Liverpool Council', https://humanists.uk/2020/08/10/faith-based-school-admissions-disadvantage-non-religious-and-minorities-humani sts-uk-tells-liverpool-council/

Humanists UK (2020c), 'Revealed: Number of pupils attending Church of England schools more than entire 'worshipping community', https://humanists.uk/2020/10/23/revealed-number-of-pupils-attending-church-of-england-schools-more-than-entire-worshipping-community/

Humanists UK (2021a), 'Children in care excluded from 76% of Catholic and all Jewish secondaries through admissions policies – new research', https://humanists.uk/2021/08/06/children-in-care-excluded-from-76-of-catholic-and-all-jewish-schools-through-admissions-policies-new-research/

Humanists UK (2021b), 'UK Government has no idea how many children locked out of schools because of faith admissions', https://humanists.uk/2021/07/27/uk-government-has-no-idea-how-many-children-locked-out-of-schools-because-of-faith-admissions/

IB World Schools Yearbook (no date), IB World Schools for MYP. https://www.ibyb.org/ib-world-schools-for-myp

Independent Schools Inspectorate (2022), 'Focused Compliance and Educational Quality Inspection Report for Schools with Residential Provision: The Royal Ballet School', https://www.isi.net/school/the-royal-ballet-school-7171

Jisc (2022), 'Applying the SAMR model to aid your digital transformation', www.jisc.ac.uk/guides/applying-the-samr-model

Kahloon, I. (2023), 'What's the matter with men?', *The New Yorker*, www.newyorker.com/magazine/2023/01/30/whats-the-matter-with-men

Kaufman, S. A. (1995), *At Home in the Universe: The Search for the Laws of Self-Organisation and Complexity*. Newhaven, CT: Yale University Press.

Kaufman, S. A. (2000), *Investigations*. Oxford: Oxford University Press.

Kennedy, P., (2012), 'William Gibson's Future Is Now', https://www.nytimes.com/2012/01/15/books/review/distrust-that-particular-flavor-by-william-gibson-book-review.html

Kim, Y., Austin, S., Subramanian, S., Thomas, J., Eddy, K., Franko, D., Rodgers, R., and Kawachi, I. (2018), 'Risk factors for disordered weight control behaviors among Korean adolescents: Multilevel analysis of the Korea Youth Risk Behavior Survey', *International Journal of Eating Disorders*, 51, (2), 124–138.

Langton, C. (1990), 'Computation at the edge of chaos', *Physica D*, 42, 12–37.

Lapowsky, I. (2015), 'What Schools Must Learn From LA's iPad Debacle', *Wired*, https://www.wired.com/2015/05/los-angeles-edtech/

Leckie, G. and Goldstein, H. (2019), 'The importance of adjusting for pupil background in school value added models: A study of Progress 8 and school accountability in England', *British Educational Research Journal*, 45(3), 518–537.

Lemov, D. (2015), *Teach Like a Champion 2.0*. San Francisco: Jossey-Bass.

Leslie, I. (2022), 'Paperback writer', The Ruffian, https://ianleslie.substack.com/p/paperback-writer

Lipson, M. Y. and Cooper, J. D. (2002), *Understanding and Supporting Comprehension Development in the Elementary and Middle Grades*. Boston: Houghton Mifflin.

Livingstone, I. and Hope, A. (2011), 'Next gen.: Transforming the UK into the world's leading talent hub for the video games and visual effects industries', NESTA, https://media.nesta.org.uk/documents/next_gen_wv.pdf

Livingstone, I. and Saeed, S. (2016), *Hacking the Curriculum: How Digital Skills Can Save Us from the Robots*. Woodbridge: John Catt.

Lucas, B., Claxton, G. and Spencer, E. (2012), 'Progression in creativity: Developing new forms of assessment', background paper for the OECD conference 'Educating for Innovative Societies', www.oecd.org/education/ceri/50153675.pdf

Lyons, S. (2013), 'Rethinking the Way We Learn', Virginia Magazine, https://uvamagazine. org/articles/rethinking_the_way_we_learn

MacTutor (no date), 'Quotations: Alfred North Whitehead', MacTutor, https://mathshistory. st-andrews.ac.uk/Biographies/Whitehead/quotations

Margallt, L. (2016), 'What screen time can really do to kids' brains', Psychology Today, www. psychologytoday.com/ca/blog/behind-online-behavior/201604/what-screen-time-can-really-do-kids-brains

Marland, M. (1975), *The Craft of the Classroom: A Survival Guide to Classroom Management in the Secondary School*. Portsmouth, NH: Heinemann Educational.

Mattingley, K. (2017), 'How can we improve teaching?', in D. James and I. Warwick (eds), *World Class: Tackling the Ten Biggest Challenges Facing Schools Today*. Abingdon: Routledge.

Mauran, C. (2023), 'OpenAI's GPT-4 aced all of its exams – except for these', Mashable. com, https://mashable.com/article/openai-gpt-4-exam-scores#:~:text=GPT%2D4%20d idn't%20just,scoring%20in%20the%2090th%20percentile

McCoy, S., Byrne, D. and O'Connor, P. (2021), 'Gender stereotyping in mothers' and teachers' perceptions of boys' and girls' mathematics performance in Ireland', *Oxford Review of Education*, 48, (3), 341–363.

McDonald, K. (2022), 'New study shows the striking correlation between school attendance and youth suicides', FEE Stories, https://fee.org/articles/new-study-shows-the-striking-correlation-between-school-attendance-and-youth-suicides

McKeller, P. (1957), *Imagination and Thinking*. London: Cohen and West.

McKenzie, B. (2018), 'Spotlight on the gender pay gap in Australia', Gender Pay Gap Series – no. 8. https://www.bakermckenzie.com/-/media/files/insight/publications/2018/ 06/spotlight-on-the-gender-pay-gap-in-australia.pdf?la=en

Meland, A. T. and Kaltvedt, E. H. (2019), 'Tracking gender in kindergarten', *Early Child Development and Care*, 189, (1), 94–103.

Morrison, N. (2022), 'Teen suicides fell during lockdown, rose when in-person schooling resumed, study finds', *Forbes*, www.forbes.com/sites/nickmorrison/2022/12/28/ teen-suicides-fell-during-lockdown-rose-when-in-person-schooling-resu med-study-finds/?sh=4615263064d7

National Secular Society (2022), 'NSS backs reduction in religious selection at Suffolk faith schools', https://www.secularism.org.uk/news/2022/02/nss-backs-reduction-in-religi ous-selection-at-suffolk-faith-schools.

Neiman, S. (2023), 'The true Left is not woke', UnHerd, https://unherd.com/2023/03/ the-true-left-is-not-woke

Newcombe, T. (2015), 'What went wrong with L.A. Unified's iPad program?', GovTech Center for Digital Education, www.govtech.com/education/what-went-wrong-with-la-unifieds-ipad-program.html

Newlan, O. (2018), 'Child mental health referrals up 26% in five years, says report', BBC News, www.bbc.co.uk/news/health-45748562

Newton, P. (2021), 'Learning during the pandemic: Quantifying lost learning', Ofqual, www. gov.uk/government/publications/learning-during-the-pandemic/learning-during-the-pandemic-quantifying-lost-time--2

Norrish, J. and Seligman, M.E.P. (2015), *Positive Education: The Geelong Grammar School Journey*. Oxford: Oxford University Press.

Nuthall, G. (2007), *The Hidden Lives of Learners*. Wellington, N.Z.: NZCER Press.

OECD (2009), 'Comparative child well-being across the OECD', in *Doing Better for Children*, www.oecd.org/social/family/43570328.pdf

OECD (2015), *Students, Computers and Learning: Making the Connection*. Paris: PISA, OECD Publishing.

Office of the Schools Adjudicator (OSA) (2022), 'Office of the Schools Adjudicator Annual Report 1 January 2021 to 31 December 2021' https://assets.publishing.service.gov.uk/government/uploads/system/uploads/attachment_data/file/1065162/OSA_annual_report_2021.pdf

Ofsted (2019), 'Education inspection framework (EIF)', www.gov.uk/government/publications/education-inspection-framework

Ofsted (2021a), 'Ofsted Parents Annual Survey 2021: Parents' awareness and perceptions of Ofsted', YouGov, https://assets.publishing.service.gov.uk/government/uploads/system/uploads/attachment_data/file/987970/Ofsted_Parents_Annual_Survey_2021.pdf

Ofsted (2021b), 'Non-association independent schools inspections and outcomes as at 31 August 2021', www.gov.uk/government/statistics/non-association-independent-schools-inspections-and-outcomes-in-england-august-2021/non-association-independent-schools-inspections-and-outcomes-as-at-31-august-2021

OpenAI (2022), 'Introducing ChatGPT', https://openai.com/blog/chatgpt

Orwell, G. (1949), *Nineteen Eighty-Four*. London: Secker and Warburg.

Owolade, T. (2022), 'Black kids should study Larkin', UnHerd, https://unherd.com/2022/06/black-kids-should-study-larkin

Pacioli, L. (1494), *Summa de Arithmetica, Geometria, Proportioni et Proportionalita*. Venice: Paganini.

Pahlke, E., Hyde, J. S., and Allison, C. M. (2014), 'The effects of single-sex compared with coeducational schooling on students' performance and attitudes: A meta-analysis', *Psychol Bull* 140, (4), 1042–72.

Peterson, Jordan. (2018), *12 Rules for Life: An Antidote to Chaos*. London: Penguin.

Planck, M. (1950), *Scientific Autobiography and Other Papers*. London: Williams and Norgate.

Plato (380 B.C.E), *Ion*. Translated by B. Jowett, http://classics.mit.edu/Plato/ion.html.

Rabbitt, M. (2023), 'Millions of Men Are in Crisis—and It's Time We Talk About It, Says Scholar Richard Reeves. Here's How to Start', https://www.mariashriversundaypaper.com/millions-of-men-are-in-crisis-and-its-time-we-talk-about-it-says-scholar-richard-reeves-heres-how-to-start/

Ravitch, D. (2017), '5 risks posed by the increasing misuse of technology in schools', EdSurge, www.edsurge.com/news/2017-12-29-5-risks-posed-by-the-increasing-misuse-of-technology-in-schools

Rawson, K. A. and Kintsch, W. (2005), 'Rereading effects depend on time of test', *Journal of Educational Psychology*, 97, (1), 70–80.

Reeves, R. (2023), 'Why boys and men?', https://ofboysandmen.substack.com/p/why-boys-and-men

Richland, L. E., Bjork, R. A., Finley, J. R. and Linn, M. C. (2005), 'Linking cognitive science to education: Generation and interleaving effects', in Bara, B. G., Barsalou, M. and Bucciarelli, L. (eds) *Proceedings of the Twenty-Seventh Annual Conference of the Cognitive Science Society*. Mahwah, NJ: Lawrence Erlbaum Associates.

Richmond, T. and Regan, E. (2023), 'Examining exams: Are there credible alternatives to written examinations?', EDSK, https://www.edsk.org/wp-content/uploads/2023/04/EDSK-Examining-exams.pdf

Riggers-Piehl, T., Lim, G. and King, K. (2018), 'Fostering Academic and Social Engagement: An Investigation into the Effects of All-Girls Education in the Transition to University', https://heri.ucla.edu/pub/NCGS-ResearchReport_final.pdf

Riverdale. (no date), 'Experiential Education', https://www.riverdale.edu/why-riverdale/experiential-education/

Robinson, K. (1999), 'All our futures: Creativity, culture and education', National Advisory Committee on Creative and Cultural Education, https://www.creativitycultureeducation.org/publication/all-our-futures-creativity-culture-and-education/

Robinson, K. (2006), 'Do schools kill creativity?', www.youtube.com/watch?v=iG9CE55wbtY

Robinson, K. (2019), 'Standardisation broke education. Here's how we can fix our schools', *Wired UK*, https://www.wired.co.uk/article/education-personalisation

Robinson, K. and Aronica, L. (2015), *Creative Schools: The Grassroots Revolution that's Transforming Education*. New York: Viking.

Robinson, M. (2023a), [*X, formerly Twitter*], 23 March 2023, @Trivium21c, https://twitter.com/Trivium21c/status/1638947274918076422?s=20

Robinson, M. (2023b), 'How do we know our curriculum is any good?', SecEd, www.sec-ed.co.uk/best-practice/how-do-we-know-our-curriculum-is-any-good-school-education-lessons-extra-curricular-classrooms/#.ZCKPa-RGpLs.twitter

Roediger III, H. L. and Karpicke, J. D. (2006), 'Test-enhanced learning: Taking memory tests improves long-term retention', *Psychological Science*, 17, 249–255.

Rohrer, D., Dedrick, R. F. and Stershic, S. (2015), 'Interleaved practice improves mathematics learning', *Journal of Educational Psychology*, 107, 900–908.

Rohrer, D. and Taylor, K. (2006), 'The effects of overlearning and distributed practice on the retention of mathematics knowledge', *Applied Cognitive Psychology*, 20, 1209–1224.

Rosanoff, M.A. (1932), 'Edison in his laboratory', *Harper's Magazine*, https://harpers.org/archive/1932/09/edison-in-his-laboratory/

Rousseau, J.-J. (1762), *Emile: Or On Education*. London: J.M. Dent.

RSA (2010), 'Changing Education Paradigms', https://www.youtube.com/watch?v=zDZFcDGpL4U

Rubel, L. (2022), [*X formerly Twitter*], 18 September 2022, @Laurie_Rubel, https://twitter.com/Laurie_Rubel/status/1571428373125021696?s=20

Satell, G. (2018), 'Set the conditions for anyone on your team to be creative'. *Harvard Business Review*, https://hbr.org/2018/12/set-the-conditions-for-anyone-on-your-team-to-be-creative

Scheerens, J. and Bosker, R. J. (1997), *The Foundations of Educational Effectiveness*. Oxford: Pergamon.

Schleicher, A. (2012), 'The case for 21st-century learning', OECD, https://web-archive.oecd.org/2012-06-14/61660-thecasefor21st-centurylearning.htm

Schneider, J. and Berkshire, J. (2020), *A Wolf at the Schoolhouse Door: The Dismantling of Public Education and the Future of School*. New York: The New Press.

Scott, B. (2023), 'The academic challenge', in D. James and J. Lunnon (eds) *The State of Independence: Key Challenges Facing Private Schools Today* (2nd ed). London: Routledge.

Seldon, A. (2022), 'It's time for educators to embrace the powers of AI and virtual reality', *The Times*, Education Commission Summit, www.thetimes.co.uk/article/its-time-to-embrace-the-powers-of-ai-and-virtual-reality-fnl0zj80q

Shakespeare, W. (1810), *As You Like it: A Comedy*. London: S. Gosnell.

Sherrington, T. (2018), 'The timeless wisdom of sitting in rows', Teacherhead, https://teacherhead.com/2018/01/31/the-timeless-wisdom-of-sitting-in-rows

Sherrington, T. (2019), 'Revisiting Dylan Wiliam's five brilliant formative assessment strategies, Teacherhead, https://teacherhead.com/2019/01/10/revisiting-dylan-wiliams-five-brilliant-formative-assessment-strategies

Sherrington, T. (2021), 'Some thoughts on grade inflation,' Teacherhead, https://teacherhead.com/2021/08/16/some-thoughts-on-exams-and-grade-inflation/

Shulman, R. D. (2020), 'This is what happens when we close doors on creativity in the classroom', *Forbes*, www.forbes.com/sites/robynshulman/2020/03/10/this-is-what-happens-when-we-close-doors-on-creativity-in-the-classroom/?sh=1dc8bd79151e

Smith, J. (2000), *The Learning Game: A Teacher's Inspirational Story*. Great Britain: Little, Brown.

Smith, S. (1810), 'Review of advice to young ladies on the improvement of the mind, by Thomas Broadhurst', in *The Works of the Rev. Sydney Smith* (vol. 1) (1840). London: Longman, Brown, Green Roberts.

Stanley, L., Tanner, W., Treadwell, J. and Blagden, J. (2022), 'The kids aren't alright: Why young people are detaching from democratic and social norms – and what to do about it', Onward, www.ukonward.com/wp-content/uploads/2022/09/kids-arent-alright-democracy.pdf

Stannard, K. (2021), 'Why (and how) girls thrive in girls-only schools: The GDST perspective', Girls' Day School Trust, www.gdst.net/wp-content/uploads/2019/08/Girls-only-schools-GDST-Perspective-2021.pdf

Strauss, V. (2015), 'Sir Ken Robinson has a lot to say about U.S. school reform (it isn't good)', *Washington Post*, www.washingtonpost.com/news/answer-sheet/wp/2015/04/21/sir-ken-robinson-has-a-lot-to-say-about-u-s-school-reform-it-isnt-good

Strauss, V. (2020), 'No, public schools are not modeled after factories. Here's why Betsy DeVos keeps saying they are', *Washington Post*, www.washingtonpost.com/education/2020/12/11/no-public-schools-are-not-modeled-after-factories-heres-why-betsy-devos-keeps-saying-they-are

Strycharczyk, D. and Zalums, L. (2021), 'Am I Lucky or just Mentally Tough…or both?', AQR International, https://aqrinternational.co.uk/am-i-lucky-or-just-mentally-tough-or-both

Tech Nation (2021), *Diversity and Inclusion in UK Tech.*, https://technation.io/diversity-and-inclusion-in-uk-tech/#key-statistics

The Guardian (2019), 'The Guardian view on creativity in schools: a missing ingredient', *The Guardian*, https://www.theguardian.com/commentisfree/2019/oct/18/the-guardian-view-on-creativity-in-schools-a-missing-ingredient

The Hound (2023), 'Social media is taking a calamitous toll on young people's mental health', Reaction, https://reaction.life/social-media-is-taking-a-calamitous-toll-on-young-peoples-mental-health

The School Run (2023), 'What is a faith school?', https://www.theschoolrun.com/what-faith-school

The Telegraph (2010), 'Schoolboys "learn better if they are allowed to walk around in class"', *The Telegraph*, https://www.telegraph.co.uk/education/educationnews/7030239/Schoolboys-learn-better-if-they-are-allowed-to-walk-around-in-class.html

The Time Education Commission (2022), 'The skills children need for life are obvious – we just need to teach them', Times Education Commission, https://www.thetimes.co.uk/article/times-education-commission-the-skills-children-need-for-life-are-obvious-we-just-need-to-teach-them

Thompson, D. (2022), 'Why American teens are so sad', *The Atlantic*, www.theatlantic.com/newsletters/archive/2022/04/american-teens-sadness-depression-anxiety/629524/?utm_source=substack&utm_medium=email

Tidman, Z. (2022), Vulnerable children wait almost three years to access mental health care while others seen in just a week. The Independent, https://www.independent.co.uk/news/health/child-mental-health-waiting-times-b1972830.html

Timimi, Z. and Timimi, S. (2022), 'Psychiatrisation of school children: Secondary school teachers' beliefs and practices on mental health and illness', in M. Harbusch (ed) *Troubled Persons Industries: The Expansion of Psychiatric Categories Beyond Psychiatry*. Palgrave Macmillan.

UNESCO (2022), 'Leave no child behind: Global report on boys' disengagement from education', https://doi.org/10.54675/BDLL3314

Villasante, T. R. (1994), *Las Ciudades Hablan: Identidades y Movimientos Sociales en Seis Metrópolis Latinoamericanas*. South America: Editorial Nueva Sociedad.

Wang, C. (2022), [*X formerly Twitter*], 1 December 2022, @corry_wang, https://twitter.com/corry_wang/status/1598176074604507136

Weinstein, B. (2021), [*X formerly Twitter*], 19 September 2021, @WeinsteinEdu, https://twitter.com/WeinsteinEdu/status/1439663925818269696

West, E. (2023), 'The modern cruelty of schools', Wrong Side of History, www.edwest.co.uk/p/the-modern-cruelty-of-schools

Wexler, N. (2018), 'Mark Zuckerberg's plan to "personalize" learning rests on shaky ground', *Forbes*, www.forbes.com/sites/nataliewexler/2018/04/19/mark-zuckerbergs-plan-to-personalize-learning-rests-on-shaky-ground/?sh=40993b923bfe

Wiliam, D. (2001), 'Level Best? Levels of attainment in national curriculum assessment Report 2001', Association of Teachers and Lecturers.

Wiliam, D. (2011), *Embedded Formative Assessment*. Bloomington: Solution Tree Press.

Wiliam, D. (2021), [*X formerly Twitter*], 27 September 2021, @dylanwiliam, https://twitter.com/dylanwiliam/status/1442590272370606080

Wiliam, D., and Thompson, M. (2008), 'Integrating assessment with instruction: What will it take to make it work?' In C. A. Dwyer (Ed.), *The future of assessment: Shaping teaching and learning* (pp. 53–82). Mahwah, NJ: Lawrence Erlbaum Associates.

Willingham, D. T. (2010), *Why Don't Students Like School? A Cognitive Scientist Answers Questions About How the Mind Works and What It Means for Your Classroom*. San Francisco: Jossey-Bass.

Willingham, D. T. (2012), *When Can You Trust the Experts? How to Tell Good Science from Bad in Education*. San Francisco: Jossey-Bass.

Wolf, G. (1996), 'Steve Jobs: The next insanely great thing', *Wired*, www.wired.com/1996/02/jobs-2

Index